PENSIONS SIMPLIFIED
7th Edition

This book is thoroughly updated, following the 2010 Budgets

Tony Granger

2000

This edition first published in 2010 by Management Books 2000 Ltd
Forge House, Limes Road
Kemble, Cirencester
Gloucestershire, GL7 6AD, UK
Tel: 0044 (0) 1285 771441
Fax: 0044 (0) 1285 771055
E-mail: info@mb2000.com
Web: www.mb2000.com

British Library Cataloguing in Publication Data is available

ISBN 9781852526443

Contents

Contents

Contents

About the Author

Tony Granger has been a retirement specialist and financial planner for more than 25 years. He was instrumental in forming the first Annuity Bureau to get the best open market option pension and annuity deals for clients, and has developed many new pensions products. He is the author of many publications and books, including *How to Finance Your Retirement* (Random House/Century), *Wealth Strategies for Your Business* (Random House/Century), *EIS and VCT Investors' Guide* (30 Day Publishing), *Independent Financial Advice and Fee-Based Financial Planning* and the *Retirement Planning Workstation* (30 Day Publishing) which includes booklets on 'Annuities', 'Pensions' and 'Estate Planning', *School and University Fees Simplified* (Management Books 2000), *Inheritance Tax Simplified* (Management Books 2000), *Business Protection Simplified* (Management Books 2000) and *Succession Planning Simplified* (Management Books 2000).

He has campaigned for many years for a better deal for those saving for retirement and has developed innovative retirement planning products to increase income and capital in retirement.

Tony is a member of the Institute of Financial Planning UK and holds the CFP, the certified financial planner certificate, as well as degrees in law and commerce from Rhodes University. He is a past president of the Institute of Life and Pensions Advisers (Financial Planning Institute) of South Africa, and a member of the Professional Finance Society (PFS).

Preface

2010 was graced with the arrival of two budgets, one on 24th March, the other the Emergency Budget of 22nd June 2010. Much of what was proposed was confirmation of the April 2009 Budget which was momentous for the pensions industry and savings generally. Given against the backdrop of the worst economic turmoil in living memory, with the global credit crunch, falling investment markets on all fronts, falling house prices, decimated investment portfolios, and the lowest bank base rate in over 300 years at 0.5%, there was little to cheer for the consumer. Enter the Government stage left with budget proposals that continue to attack and target those who wish to build up savings for retirement, with higher taxes and restrictive pension funding contribution levels. These new measures are mainly aimed at the higher earners; however, those same high earners often control employer pension schemes, and their personal decision-making could have a knock-on effect all around. This will certainly be the case with final salary (defined benefit) schemes, which are becoming fewer in number every month.

The withdrawal of personal allowances, in the 2009 Budget, for taxpayers at £100,000 taxable income on a £1 for £2 basis from 2010/11 (effectively an increase in the tax rate), a new income tax rate of 50% from 6th April 2010, a restriction of contributions for higher earners earning £150,000+ from all sources – will mean that for some, not only will the pension pot be less, but also the funds received by way of pensions or annuities will decrease because of higher taxation.

Stockmarket and investment falls that have generated losses for pension funds in recent years will increase the pressure on funding at adequate levels to make up the shortfalls experienced. In addition, those in income drawdown, unless their funds are protected, will have experienced capital depletion if maintaining their income levels. Some pension funds have lost 50% or more in value, and will take years to recover. Whilst annuities may, in many cases, provide less income than the maximum GAD (Government Actuary's Department) rates allow for drawdown, they are certainly proving to be the safer bet for many.

The pensions industry focus is currently on the new compulsory NEST pensions regime for all businesses expected to begin implementation in 2012. Adequate schemes need to be in place at least 6 months before that date, although the new regime will be phased in gradually. Whilst there are opt-outs available (for example, if you already have a pension fund with adequate contributions), employers will have to contribute at least 3%, employees 4% and the state, by way of tax relief, a further 1%. Employees contribute on a band basis – employers on a full earnings basis.

Four years on from 'A Day' (6th April 2006), we have seen many changes to pensions legislation, some of it to reduce the administrative burden brought on by a consolidation of the pensions regime under pensions simplification; getting to grips with new terms such as USP and ASP, and new planning techniques to reduce the incidence of inheritance tax on pension funds, and the considerable new thought that goes into investment planning within pension schemes, especially those schemes in income drawdown. The challenge remains for sufficient income to be created from investments without capital depletion, and the preservation of capital.

Our investment planning as financial advisers and planners has changed accordingly. The segmentation of pension funds for growth on the one hand (without necessarily having to provide for income through capital depletion) and income-producing investments has gone further than variable term annuities, as people seek not only low volatility but also non-correlation to the stock market and interest rate movements.

Given a blank sheet of paper to map out a beneficial pensions landscape, I have come to the realisation that pensions simplification has merely played with the rules and regulations governing pensions, and does not tackle the major issues of how to get people to save more for their retirement, when they will be living longer and possibly spending as much time in retirement as they did during their working lives. Sadly we have obsolete Government thinking on what Society wants for its pensioners and those working towards a successful retirement, including providing for today's dependants and tomorrow's children. The new Coalition Government has announced various consultations affecting pensions, the most immediate being a raising of the age to 77 under USP (from 75) before having to take an annuity or tax free cash.

Everyone is aware that the State can only do so much. The State pension scheme is unfunded. That means that national insurance contributions will increase heavily as the retirees living longer outnumber those in work in the future. There should be employer compulsion without opt-outs; there should be the ability to pass the balance of your pension funds on death to other generations (to your children to help with their pensions, or even your parents to help with rising long-term care costs as they live longer) without penal taxation – up to 82% of your remaining funds can be taxed on death, unless they pass to a charity.

Generous in funding allowances (HMRC will contribute £20 for every £80 contributed by individuals, with tax reliefs at a further 20% of their net contribution for higher rate taxpayers) and corporate tax relief for employers; funds that grow tax free, funds that allow for 25% in tax free cash – the funding and investment growth environment for pensions is without parallel. However, the eventual distribution mechanism fails us, and with it the opportunity to reduce reliance on the State Pensions scheme and benefit system well into the future.

To truly build retirement and pensions wealth, involving families, would mean a total rethink. The counter-arguments made by the State will be the loss to the treasury of taxation revenues on the one hand, and the argument by the life offices that annuities and pensions are based on a risk pooling system of winners and losers and they have to manage that outcome (some people die too soon, others live too long). Yet in some countries, the

13

unused annuity surpluses are paid to the deceased's estate, so it can be done.

State pensions ages are increasing for women to age 65, gradually from 2010 (from age 60), and the new state pension age for men and women will be age 65, affecting all women born after 5th April 1955. Women born after April 1950 and before April 1955 will now have a state pension age of between 60 and 65. The state pension age was to rise to age 68 by 2046, however, the gradual increase in female state pension age to 65 begins from the start of the 2010/11 tax year. It should be fully equalised by April 2020 with the men's SPA (state pension age).

Employers are moving away from final salary schemes (defined benefit, or 'DB') towards defined contribution schemes (DC) because of costs, and are most unlikely to increase pension funding if they can help it. People must be encouraged to provide for their retirement years, because the old certainties are not so certain any more.

The major objective for most people will be to ensure a successful retirement, and a plan of action will show how best to build it.

Retirement planning is not just about pensions, but about building a savings plan that includes pensions. It is not only about what has been done or accomplished in the past, but what can be accomplished in the future.

Knowing your way around the pensions maze, avoiding the major pitfalls and traps that will cost you time as well as money and knowing how to manipulate the system can significantly increase your pension's wealth and retirement success.

This book is about how to beat the system, and also how to understand the complex issues to make it easier to accumulate pensions wealth in uncertain times.

This book is thoroughly updated following the March 2010 Budget and the June 1010 Emergency Budget.

Please take professional advice before acting, as the author and publishers cannot be held responsible for your acts or omissions. The value of investments, including pensions, may go down as well as up and you may lose your capital. Always consider all the options before considering a certain course of action, as your risk profile and personal circumstances may change. If loans are taken against property or fixed assets, you could lose your capital if interest payments are not kept up and loan terms are not adhered to.

Tony Granger
July 2010

14

Key 2010 Budget Changes

24th March Budget 2010

For 2010/11

- Annual Allowance for pension contributions rises to £255,000 per person per year and frozen to 2015/16.

- Lifetime allowance rises to £1.8 million and is frozen to 2015/16.

- Personal allowance is withdrawn at £1 for every £2 of income above £100,000

- Additional rate of tax of 50% on taxable income over £150,000, and an additional rate on dividend income of 42.5%.

- From 2010/11 the ISA savings limits were increased to £10,200 each per tax year (of which £5,100 can be in cash). The limits are to rise with the RPI from April 2011.

- The National Employment Savings Trust (NEST) to register with HMRC for pension contribution relief.

- Under Pensions Act 2008 employers have a duty to ensure all employees are active members of a pension scheme, with automatic enrolment planned for 2012, and be legally obliged to make contributions on behalf of employees. No tax charge on loans from a pension scheme to fund the new NEST arrangement.

- Confirmation of previous budgets that from 2011/12 tax relief on pension contributions for individuals with income over £150,000 will be gradually tapered. At £180,000 you will only receive basic rate relief (20%) on contributions. Total income is before deduction for pension contributions and charitable donations. If your income is £130,000 and over and together with your employer pension contributions takes you to £150,000 or over, your pension tax reliefs will be tapered. Anti-forestalling measures came into effect for 2009/10 and 2010/11 to prevent pension contribution increases before the new rules came into effect. The special annual allowance of £20,000 - £30,000 (depending on your circumstances) should cease to apply *after* the 2010/11 tax year (as the tapered pension relief rates come in then).

- The inheritance tax nil rate band is frozen at £325,000 to 6 April 2015.

22nd June 2010 Budget

- Personal tax allowances frozen at 2009/10 rates for 2010/11

- Increases in personal allowance for those under age 65 by £1,000 to £7,475 in 2011/12

- Capital gains tax on gains after 22.6.2010, for individuals a new higher rate of 28% where total taxable income and gains are above £37,400 – the higher rate applies to gains exceeding the limit. The personal allowance and losses reduce the gain. Where total taxable income and gains do not exceed the limit, gains remain taxable at 18%. For trustees and personal representatives, all taxable gains are taxed at 28%.

- Entrepreneur's relief is increased to £5 million from 23.6.2010 (the previous budget increased this to £2 million), and gains above that are taxed at 10%.

- The Government confirms the restrictions to pension contribution relief in the Finance Act 2010 for 2011/12 onwards by high income individuals. The Government is considering reducing the pension annual allowance from £255,000 to a range of £30,000 to £40,000.

- From 2011/12 the need to buy an annuity by age 75 moves to age 77; income drawdown limits will also extend to age 77; IHT charges where a member dies on or after age 75 will also be affected. In other words, the USP band will move to age 77, and ASP will be from age 77 from 6.4.2012. These are interim measures whilst a consultation process commences.

- The National Employment Savings Trust (NEST) – which is the new name for the employee compulsory pensions savings scheme (formerly Personal Accounts) will allow tax relief for employee and employer contributions from the date of the next Finance Act.

- The Government is considering removing the default retirement age of 65, but this will not be before 2011.

- **State Pension**

Claimant	£97.65 per week (£5077.80 p.a.)
Adult dependant	£58.50 per week (£3042 p.a.)
Total married	£156.15 per week (£8,119.80p.a.)

- The basic state pension increases by 2.5% from April 2010. The Government confirmed a triple guarantee for the basic state pension. From April 2010 it will be increased by the higher of the increase in prices, earnings or 2.5%.

- **Pensions Credit** if married or civil partnership.
  Guarantee Credit
  Single   £132.60   (£6,895.20 pa)
  Couple   £202.40   (£10,524.80)

Post Budget Key Announcement 15th July 2010

The Government announces it proposed to end the rules forcing pension investors to buy an annuity at a specific age. This will take effect from 6th April 2011. It proposes capped and flexible drawdown options before and after age 75, making it unnecessary to offer alternatively secured pensions (ASP). There may even be tax free cash in excess of 25% so long as a minimum income is secured to prevent pensioners running out of funds. Announcements were also made on taxation of funds on death pre and post age 75, and inheritance tax applying to funds.

From the 2009 Budget relevant to this tax year 2010/11

- There is an increase in the upper earnings limit for class 1 and class 4 national insurance contributions from £770 to £844 per week. This affects rebates to pension schemes and calculations for salary sacrifice for pension contribution purposes. [same for 2010/11]

- For the contracted-out rebate on a salary-related scheme, the employee rate is 1.6% and employer rate is 3.7%; for a money purchase scheme it is 1.6% for employee and 1.4% for employer. The rebate is to £770 per week. [£97.01 to £770 in 2010/11]

- NI contribution tax rises from 11% to 11.5% for individuals from April 2011.

- Higher rate income tax relief on pension contributions will be abolished from 2011/12 tax year. If earning over £150,000, above that level tax relief tapers to £180,000 where basic rate tax relief applies.

- There are interim measures for the 2009/10 tax year through a Special Annual Charge of 20%. This applies if your income exceeds £150,000 in this tax year, *or in any of the two previous tax years*. Income for this purpose is total income for the tax year before pension contributions, personal allowances, or any other reliefs or deductions (gross income from all sources). You can deduct reliefs such as trading losses, including deductions for pension contributions up to a maximum of £20,000, less any gift aid deductions. You then add any income foregone by a salary sacrifice arrangement in return for pension contributions entered into on or after 22nd April 2009. Contributions paid before 23rd April 2009 are excluded from the 2009/10 tax year.

- The Special Annual Allowance (SAA) is £20,000 per year. This includes employer's contributions and defined benefit scheme accrual (calculated in the same way as a Pension Input amount for Annual Allowance purposes). Any input in excess of the SAA will be subject to the SAA charge of 20%. Existing tax reliefs continue to be available to all whose input amount in a tax year is £20,000 or less.

- There are two exemptions: (i) where regular contributions currently exceed £20,000 p.a. – *no* SAA charge if regular premiums continue to be paid, and must be paid at least quarterly to qualify as regular contributions, and (ii) where the member retires on the grounds of ill health or dies before the end of the tax year.

- From 22nd April 2009 UK investors with distributions from offshore funds with more than 40% in equities will receive a non-payable dividend tax credit. (This reinstates the tax credit for offshore funds announced in the 2008 budget). Basic rate taxpayers will pay no further tax. Higher rate taxpayers will be liable to a further 25% income tax based on the net dividend received. If however, the offshore fund is invested in more than 60% in interest-bearing assets, no tax credit is available. In this case the distribution is treated as interest and taxed at 20% for basic rate taxpayers and 40% for higher rate taxpayers. Also, individuals receiving dividends from non-resident UK companies will be entitled to a non payable tax credit (from a qualifying territory).

- From 6th April 2010 non-UK resident individuals will not qualify for UK personal allowances or reliefs by reason of being Commonwealth citizens (but may still qualify for double taxation relief). This could make pensions payable to those living abroad more expensive as more tax could be payable.

- From 6th April 2009 EIS tax relief can be related back to the previous tax year at 100%. So if the maximum £500,000 was invested, income tax relief of £100,000 can be related back to the previous tax year. Investments need no longer be made by 6th October in the tax year. This may help high earners, who will be limited in their pension contributions in the future to seek additional tax reliefs.

1

The Changing Pensions Landscape

The Green and White Papers • the Turner Report • pensions simplification • the Pensions Act 2007 • the Finance Act 2007 • the Pre-Budget Speech Oct-07, Budgets 2008, 2009, Coalition Government 2010

Pensions and pension funding have occupied Government thought at a very high level, particularly with regard to the State Pension and the state second tier pension S2P, how it is funded and paid. The current position is that the basic state pension increases by 2.5% from April 2010. The Government confirmed a triple guarantee for the basic state pension. From April 2010 it will be increased by the higher of the increase in prices, earnings or 2.5%.

The reduction in the number of qualifying years for a person reaching state pension age from 2010/11 tax year is 30 years for a full-rate basic state pension.

The accrual rate for middle and upper bands of S2P will merge into one band accruing at 10% in respect of band earnings between £14,100 and £40,040.

The gradual increase in female state pension age to 65 begins from the start of the 2010/11 tax year. It should be fully equalised by April 2020 with the men's SPA (state pension age).

The Government is considering removing the default retirement age of 65, but this will not be before 2011.

The Coalition Government is to consult on a number of issues, including the taking of an annuity from age 75 (temporary legislation is being introduced to raise the age to age 77from 2011/12 and the need to buy an annuity by age 75 moves to age 77-), and possibly to do away with ASP altogether. This is a good opportunity to totally reform the savings culture for pensions, so that the bottleneck at age 75, and penal IHT and other taxes on pensions are totally removed, so as to introduce a non-restricted retirement savings culture. Other consultations will be on reducing the annual funding limits from £255,000 to £30,000- £45,000. This is another retrograde step in my opinion. People should be encouraged to save as much as possible without penalty (right now you pay a penal tax of 55% if overfunded). However, tax relief can be limited to a particular level – but don't penalise those who wish to build pension funds for themselves and their families. The Government appears once again to be too pre-occupied with the mechanics and not the benefits, or target benefit saving. Pensions are the culture for retirement, and the focus should be on making them work efficiently. This was Simplification was all about in 2006 – well intentioned, but a complete nightmare to administer, let alone motivate to clients. Every successive round of budgets and supporting legislation throws up more 'blockers' to an efficient system.

Up to 2006 there were various consultations – the Green Paper, the White paper and the Turner report.

Government consultation and the Turner Report have resulted in some changes brought about largely through the change in the 'A' Day pension regimes. Some of the issues first mooted below, have been addressed and now appear in modified format.

The Government continues with its own simplification programme, and the much-heralded Green Paper on pensions proposed that the Government addresses a range of issues:

* the problem caused by the increase in the number of people expected to live beyond retirement age

* people must save more and work longer

* linking the state pension to earnings would not be sustainable in the long term (this has happened from 2010 with a link to prices, earnings or 2.5%).

* plans not to scrap means-tested benefits and add them to the basic state pension

* not to raise the state retirement age – (this has not happened – it is being raised, and sooner than expected)

* people deferring the state pension voluntarily to age 70 may get a lump sum of £20,000 on top of their normal pension, £30,000 for a couple

* self-employed people to opt into the second state pension

* a need to simplify occupational pension schemes and abolish the Minimum Funding Requirement and Guaranteed Minimum Pension – (happening)

* introducing a single tax regime for pensions – (has changed)

* compulsory membership of employer schemes – (being mooted now for 2012 under NEST)

* compulsory retirement age to be scrapped – (has happened)

* allowing people to continue in work after receiving an occupational pension – (has happened)

* raising the pension age from 50 to 55 by 2010, as the minimum age from when a pension can be taken – (has happened)

- for Personal Pension Plans, individuals would be able to contribute up to £200,000 per year to their pension scheme, with a lifetime limit of £1.4 million – (has happened, with modifications, such as contributions up to £255,000 in 2010/11, and a lifetime limit of £1.8 million)
- the tax-free lump sum would remain.

Big changes are advocated for annuities allowing for 'limited period annuities' bought for a set period of time (these already exist with capital growth annuities); or 'value-protected annuities' paying out a lump sum if the holder dies before age 75. This last proposal may not go far enough, as one of the retirement fears is of losing your fund on death.

Giving more informed choice to individuals whilst simplifying pensions legislation and encouraging people to save (3 million people are seriously under-saving for retirement) within a simpler pensions framework is to be welcomed. Reform with better protections, reducing the costs of annuity guarantees (up to 65% of your fund can be lost to guarantees) and not being able to pass on much of what remains of your fund on death are now a reality.

The White Paper

The White Paper was published in May 2006 and was the most comprehensive investigation for pensions reform – 'Security in Retirement: towards a new pensions system' (see www.dwp.gov.uk/pensionsreform/whitepaper.asp). The first priority was to tackle pensioner poverty and changes have been made with pension credits, winter fuel payments and state pension increases.

The White Paper sets out proposals for the long-term future of pensions and retirement savings. It tackles private savings which are in decline, pensions adequacy, living longer in retirement, and compulsion by employers to fund for employees. In particular, the White Paper will affect occupational pensions and employees, and the Government will focus on the employer to bring about increased pensions savings. Employers will be compelled to contribute to pensions at the minimum contribution rate of 4% of salary by 2012. However, don't hold your breath – most employers will leave it until the last minute to do anything, because of cost and the resources to do so.

The second White Paper, 'Personal Accounts: A New Way to Save', sets out plans to help up to 10 million low-earners build up private savings with contributions from employers and the state.

Planned automatic enrolment from 2012 means a worker can opt out of the employer's occupational scheme and have their own private pension account. All eligible workers will be automatically enrolled into either a suitable work-based pension scheme or into a Personal Account (now NEST). The contribution will be based on a minimum of 4% of gross earnings on a band of earnings between £5,000 and £35,000 a year. These contributions will be matched by a minimum of 3% of their gross earnings by the employer and 1% by the state in the form of tax relief. The *Pensions Act 2007* created the Personal Accounts Delivery Authority to advise on Personal Accounts proposals.

Currently the largest number of employers (117,000) offering a contribution to a pension scheme is smaller companies employing 1-4 people. 983,000 companies contribute nothing to their employees' pensions. (Mintel Occupational Pensions Report, July 2006). The sad fact is that the majority of companies do not contribute towards employee pensions, which still remains a highly-regarded employee benefit.

Government White Paper proposals can be summed up as two key issues – how to encourage employers to contribute and how to encourage individuals to make pension contributions. The main proposals included a basic state pension linked to earnings, not inflation from 2012 – (the triple lock in of earnings, prices or 2.5% is operative from April 2010); rebates to defined contribution schemes ceasing in 2011/2012; a rise in the state pension age from 66 in 2024 to 68 by 2046 – this is now shortened to 2024 ; a reduction in the qualifying years for a state pension to 30 years from 2010 (this has happened); from 2012 the Government offers a low-cost savings account to employees with a 4% contribution from employees and 3% from employers, and 1% from tax relief – this is happening now with NEST. With this comes the fact that people will work longer and require more flexibility in retirement and investing their pensions savings.

Turner Report

There are two key recommendations in the Turner Report. This is an appraisal of current pension provision – essentially people not having enough from the state pensions to live on. The first is a low-cost National Pensions Savings Scheme (NPSS) – now known as NEST – a one-size-fits-all national pensions arrangement (as opposed to the ABI proposal for 'partnership pensions' run by insurers with a choice of options). This will be a new system of personal pension accounts to encourage people to save, and where employers must contribute 3% to the scheme by 2012. The employee will contribute 4% and 1% will come from tax relief, making it 8% of earnings on a contribution between earnings of £5,000 and £33,500.

Benefits would be an annuity but no tax-free lump sum, and on death, the fund would fall into the member's estate. Fund management charges would be as low as 0.3% per annum.

The introduction of the NPSS (now NEST) could lead to a reduction in funding existing schemes, with employers only contributing the minimum amount to the NPSS (NEST). The idea is to make pensions cheaper and simpler through auto-enrolment (if an employee is not currently in a scheme) and compulsory employer contributions. What will certainly be required is better employee communications, making pensions easier to understand. Why wait until 2012 to implement these proposals? – at the time, it was commented that a four-year delay in starting pension savings will reduce pension income by at least 25%. The delay could cut future pension income for a 30-year old by as much as 39% (Scottish Equitable).

The second recommendation is for state pensions reform with a less means-tested but more generous state pension scheme and the phasing out of contracting-out from the S2P (second tier state pension scheme).

Pensions simplification – the benefits

Pensions simplification came into force from the 6th April 2006, and implements the *Finance Act 2004*. The main benefits after many years of consultation and review, are:

- to reduce the complexity of the current system

- make retirement plans more flexible

- to have a single simple allowance on the size of the pension fund that can be accumulated by any individual

- to expand the range of investment options available, with more choice

- to consolidate and integrate occupational and personal pension plan rules

- more generous contribution allowances than previously

- greater flexibility at retirement, without having to take an annuity

- annuities that provide for unused funds to be returned to an estate or beneficiaries on death (value protected annuities) but now after penal taxation

- greater drawdown options of pension benefits as income, leading to an ongoing accumulation of pension assets

- passing on a pension fund on death (although there are inheritance tax and other tax issues)

- greater opportunities to transfer to another scheme – there will be increased portability amongst different schemes

- greater pension scheme choice – you can now hold an occupational pension and a personal pension plan simultaneously, for greater diversification

- you can draw a pension and carry on working – you don't have to retire from your job

- the *fear factor* of not making pension contributions because:
  (i) the state will provide
  (ii) you lose your pension assets on death
  (iii) you may be forced to take an annuity which doesn't pay very much
     ... and other concerns may now diminish as:
     (a) we know the state will only ever provide the smallest, most basic pension benefits
     (b) your pension funds can now continue for beneficiaries after death
     (c) and even annuity values can be protected.
  The biggest fear of whether you can trust your employer to manage and protect your pension fund, unfortunately still remains.

- to plan for your pension and pension funds to outlive you, not the other way around is possible with greater flexibility

- more active pension fund management is possible – your money and funds must last longer than ever before

- the ability to assist family members to build a 'family' pension fund to help future generations is now a possibility; you benefit from it as well as spouse/partner and children (however, at present, only if you help individually fund their pensions).

Blockers giving rise to non-funding of pensions

I call them 'blockers' for they are reasons that prevent people from being committed to saving for their retirement through pension plans. Much of what has occurred in the past gives rise to a negative mental attitude that may be difficult to change. The Government believes it is removing barriers to entry and over-regulation of the pensions industry whilst introducing a positive environment to save for retirement. Individuals know they must save for a financially secure retirement, but have suffered in the past from over-expensive pension product providers on plan charges; from mistrust of employers and pension scheme trustees; poorly performing pension fund investments; lack of flexibility and – the big one – uncertainty as to what happens to their lifetime funds on death.

We also have unscrupulous financial advisers giving the wrong advice, and unwitting consumers taking that advice. People have transferred from good final salary schemes to poorly performing personal pension schemes; many have contracted out of the state's second tier pension scheme – formerly SERPS, now the S2P – and should be contracting back in.

The inability of some employers to protect their pension funds and their members when the employer gets into financial trouble and the lack of safety for a secure retirement is a major issue – and probably the single main reason why employees do not take up pension schemes offered by their employers – even if non-contributory, may well be solved through funding into the employee's own choice of pension plan account.

The cost of pension contributions affects those with limited incomes; as does the fact that many employees change jobs more often now than they used to. Consumer attitudes can change, and they do. The new pensions reforms should have given clarity and certainty and create a savings environment in the future that will be better than we have had in the past.

The Pension Protection Fund

Established by the *Pensions Act 2004*, the Pension Protection Fund (PPF) is to protect members of final salary schemes by paying compensation should the employer become insolvent and the pension scheme under-funded, or where fraud has taken place. The PPF went live on 6th April 2005, and whilst state-backed, levies a charge on occupational schemes to provide the funds for compensation. There are now 120 final salary schemes in the Pension Protection Fund.

Those who reach retirement age, or who are in receipt of pensions will receive 100%, whilst those below that age (including those who have retired early other than for reasons of ill health) will receive 90%. The compensation is capped at a pension of £33,054.09 p.a. at age 65 in 2010/11. At the 90% cap, the maximum entitlement will be £29,748.68 p.a. in 2010/11 (from April 2010 – *Pension Compensation Cap Order 2010*). There are further limitations – for example, survivors' pensions are limited to 50% of the full entitlement.

Any form of pension fund protection is to be welcomed, although the PPF only applies to final salary schemes. Being offered a transfer out of the pension scheme to another provider (as opposed to going into the PPF) is usually preferable, because of the pension cap and the fact that you immediately lose 10% of your pension fund value when your employer fund goes in to the PPF.

Finance Act 2007

Royal Assent was received on 19th July 2007. Provisions relating to Pension schemes are in sections 68–70 and Schedules 18 to 20, where amendments are made to the *Finance Act 2004*. Section 68 and Schedule 18 remove the tax relief for personal term assurance for occupational schemes from 31st July 2007 and other pension schemes from 5th April 2007. Policies issued before the prescribed dates are protected for their existing tax reliefs. For occupational schemes this is 1st August 2007 (policy application received before 29th March 2007) and other schemes 1st August 2007 where the application was received before 14th December 2006 (where there are no pension rights under the scheme) and 13th April 2007 where pension rights were being accrued. Varying the terms of a protected policy will lose the tax reliefs. Tax relief on employer contributions is not affected by these changes (group life schemes are therefore unaffected, and continue to enjoy tax relief on contributions).

Section 69 and Schedule 19 of FA 2007 makes changes to *Finance Act 2004* and the *Inheritance Tax Act 1984* relating to alternatively secured pensions (ASPs). The minimum amount of ASP paid in an 'ASP year' to a member or dependant must be at least 55% of the 'basis amount' for that year (minimum income). If the minimum amount is not paid then this will be a scheme chargeable payment taxed at up to 40% on the difference between the minimum amount and the actual amount paid. The maximum amount of ASP payable rises from 70% to 90%.

Transfer lump sum death benefits become unauthorised after 6th April 2007 when the member or dependant dies on or after that date. In addition, the facility to guarantee an ASP for ten years is removed where the member dies on or after 6th April 2007.

Other changes have been made to ensure a consistent approach in the transition to the new regime such as (i) unauthorised payments are reduced by the amount of the scheme sanction charge (after 6th April 2007) (ii) transfers without loss of enhanced protection from the Lifetime Allowance charge are extended to include a partial transfer to a money purchase arrangement (that is not a cash balance arrangement) or a transfer from a defined benefits or cash balance arrangement to another defined benefits or cash balance arrangement made as part of a 'relevant business transfer'.

Changes to pension commencement lump sum (PCLS) (otherwise known as tax free cash)

From 6th April 2006 paragraphs 9–11 of Schedule 20 of the *Finance Act 2007* extend the period within which a PCLS may be paid free of tax to any time within an 18 month period starting 6 months before and ending 12 months after the date when the member becomes entitled to the related pension. The entitlement to the PCLS must have arisen before age 75. If you die having taken the lump sum but before taking the pension, entitlement to the lump sum is deemed to have arisen immediately before death. There is also now a 2 year time limit on the payment of lump sum death benefits of the scheme being notified of the member's death.

2010/11 - Note you must still take your tax free cash by age 75, although the taking of income, or annuity can now be deferred to age 77 from 2011/12 , following the June 22 Budget.

Unsecured pension funds (USP)

A review of the annual maximum withdrawal from USP may be permitted more frequently than every 5 years but only at the direction of the member. The maximum withdrawal requirement review remains at every 5 years. This applies on or after notifications given from 6th December 2006.

'Winding up' lump sums

The change requires conditions to be met only by the current employer, not any previous employers at the time the winding-up lump sum is paid, and applies after 6th April 2006.

Spreading of tax relief for pension contributions (PBR13)

New legislation was introduced in the *Finance Act 2008* to ensure that the rules that spread tax relief for large employer contributions relative to their contribution in the previous year cannot be circumvented (from 10th October 2007). You cannot avoid spreading of contributions by routing them through a new company. Pension contributions are tax relievable against profits (deductible to the employer company). Large contributions are spread by up to 4 years,(where it is more than 210% of the contribution paid in the previous chargeable period; and exceeds 110% of the contribution paid in that previous period by at least £500,000).

Pre-Budget Report (PBR)
Issued: 9th October 2007

The PBR of 9th October 2007 announced a number of changes. The measures proposed include legislation to ensure that individuals are unable to avoid tax charges by diverting tax-relieved pension savings into inheritance using scheme pensions and lifetime annuities, and measures to ensure that employer pension schemes are unable to avoid tax by exploiting rules which are designed to allow schemes to spread tax reliefs over a number of years.
The principal changes may be summarised as follows:

1. Pension credit

The standard minimum guarantee rises to £130 for single pensioners and £198.45 for couples in 2009/10. Every person aged over 60 will be guaranteed at least £6,760 per annum. From November 2009, the capital disregard for pension credit and pensioner-related Housing and Council Tax benefit will increase from £6,000 to £10,000. [note that from 2010/11 Pensions Credit is as follows:

Pensions Credit
Guarantee Credit
Single   £132.60   (£6,895.20 pa)
Couple   £202.40   (£10,524.80)

Savings Credit threshold
Single   £98.40
Couple   £157.25

The age of entitlement for a guarantee credit payment will gradually increase from age 60 to 65 by 2020.]

2. State second pension (S2P)

Proposals in the *Pensions Act 2007* reforms S2P to become a simple flat rate weekly top up to the basic State Pension by 2030. The Upper Accruals point for S2P is introduced from 2009 (as opposed to 2010). The upper earning limit will be frozen and renamed upper accrual point to facilitate the gradual withdrawal of the 10% accrual band.

3. Variable annuities

The Government refuses to liberalise the regime for variable annuity schemes. The maximum annuity rate required under guaranteed annuity definition rules (GAD) remains the same. This effectively prevents increased 'equity type' returns from being developed in products. You will not be able to receive a guaranteed income whilst benefiting from future investment returns, unless within overall GAD limits and lifetime funding limits.

4. Inheriting tax-relieved pension savings

PBRN 15 states that Legislation was introduced in the *Finance Act 2008* that tax-relieved pension savings diverted into inheritance using scheme pensions and lifetime annuities will be subject to unauthorised payment tax charges and possibly inheritance tax. This applies to surrenders made after 10th October 2007 and for increases in pension rights attributable to the death of a member when the member dies after 6th April 2008. Unauthorised payments are subject to income tax charges of up to 70%. Total tax payable could be 82%. The new proposed legislation will not apply where the scheme has 20 or more members and the increases in rights are applied at the same rate for each member. The charge on scheme pensions only applies to 'connected persons', namely family members or business associates. There is no charge if not connected. SSAS schemes can have a maximum of 11 members and could previously pass pension money on to families at death without paying additional tax. The new rules bring SSAS schemes into line with family SIPPs. A SSAS member, on retirement, receives an income direct from the scheme based on actuarial guidelines and is not required to buy an annuity for life using an annuity. On death the remaining assets remain in the pension fund, rather than being lost to an insurance company providing an annuity.

Previously the death of a member did not trigger a tax liability. Now the rules will penalise connected persons (family members or business associates) and schemes of under 20 members passing on pension rights to other scheme members. The tax charge is 70%, in line with tax applied to funds passed on via ASPs. Funds passed on may be liable to inheritance tax, and if the person dies after age 75 [will now be age 77 from 2011/12], could be as high as 82%. There is now a level playing field for ASP and scheme pensions. Planning could involve say an older director without family providing pensions for the rest of the workforce, or the pension funds could go back to the employer after a tax charge of 35%. Note that on death of a member his or her pension fund can still pass to a nominated spouse or civil partner and dependants without penalty where provided for under the rules.

2008 and 2009 Budgets

The first Budget in 2008 (12th March 2008) announced key changes affecting pensions and retirement planning.

The reduction of income tax rate at the basic rate level from 22% to 20% reduced the HMRC contribution to 20%, and higher rate taxpayers could claim 20% instead of 18%. The transferable nil rate band between married couples and civil partners meant that fewer pension schemes will be chargeable to IHT in the second dying's estate. Coupled with this was the IHT charge, from 6.4.2008 for unauthorised lump sum payments where death occurs after age 75. There was also an easement in the rules for trivial commutations below £2,000, and in addition to the payments of 1% of the standard lifetime allowance (in 2010/11 1% x £1.8 million = £18,000.

There was the introduction of a new authorised payments regime to avoid a 70% unauthorised tax charge on overpaid pensions or those that continued to be paid after death, as well as other pensions legislative changes.

In the 2009 Budget, we saw the first of the Government attacks on contributions to pension funds being introduced, together with anti-forestalling provisions to ensure that contributions were limited to a percentage of earnings going back two years. There was a 20% special annual charge of 20% announced for 2009/10, if your income exceeded £150,000 in the current tax year or any two previous tax years. Income foregone through salary sacrifice arrangements applied to pension benefits after 22nd April 2009 was to be added back to income. In addition, contributions were restricted to the special annual allowance of £20,000 per year (increased to £30,000 under certain circumstances). This included employer's contributions and defined benefit scheme accrual. These restrictions applied notwithstanding an annual allowance contribution cap of £245,000 in that tax year. Announcements were made for future tapering of tax relief to 20% for those with incomes over £150,000 - £180,000 per annum from 2011/12. Higher rate relief from income tax contributions to be abolished from 2011/12 (tapered from £150,000 and reaching 20% at £180,000). An announcement was made on the freezing of the annual and lifetime allowances from 2010 to 2016. A higher rate (additional rate) tax band was introduced at 50% for those earning over £150,000 and the personal allowance was reduced for earners over £100,000 (to nil at £112,950) from 2010/11. This budget was effectively an attack on pension contributions and high earners. Rises in NI contributions were also announced.

Overall then, since Pensions Simplification commenced in 2006, we have had a concerted attack by the Government aimed at pension funds in general and also targeting the high net worth. Penal taxes on your pension money if you die and funds are received by your estate; limits on the contributions you can make; restriction of contribution tax relief; increased rule-making and legislation has made the taking out, management and administration of pension funds more complicated than ever before.

For large company pension schemes, the stock market crash and credit crunch has depressed values, causing many more funds to go into deficit with being unable to fund their deficits. Pension funds must now provide for people living longer, and many will find it difficult to do so in the future. The Pension Protection Fund is set to expand as more schemes are unable to continue. However, this fund only caters for defined benefit schemes and not other schemes that may be in trouble.

The 2010 Budgets

There has been a strong focus on the State Pension scheme with the triple lock promise in respect of pension increases in the 2010 Budget. The age at which a state pension can be taken is being accelerated, and female ages will equate much sooner. Instead of bringing females into line with male retirement ages at age 65 (where one would expect equalisation), this has been extended to around age 68 by 2024.

Worryingly National Insurance contributions are on the rise, both for employers and employees. This is a trend that will continue. The reason why this is the case, is that there is no state pension fund. The workers pay in their NI contributions and the pensioners immediately draw them out as pensions. Fewer workers and more retired people mean that the NI contributions can only rise at a more rapid rate in the future.

This new Coalition Government has also managed to alienate a vast public sector worker base through having to deal with crippling public sector pension costs, and future funding.

All in all, the next few years will be an unsettling period of time for those saving for pensions and for those about to go off on pension. The old securities have long evaporated, and people must pay more attention to what they have and how to increase their retirement wealth. However, this is also an opportunity by individuals to do the best they can for themselves, and for the Government to seriously consider what pension funds are meant for, what they mean to people and families, and how to motivate savings, not destroy the incentive to save.

2

Pensions as Part of Retirement Planning

Retirement planning is the combination of pensions, savings and investments with the long-term goal of providing tax-free cash (or tax efficient cash) as well as annual income to secure a comfortable and successful retirement.

Pensions usually play a major part in retirement planning, but are not the only savings vehicles to be considered. Whilst conventional pension funds provide a tax-free investment growth vehicle during the investment term, there are numerous choices at retirement to opt for a mixture of tax-free cash and a lower pension or annuity, or to draw down an income from your pension fund to age 75 (From 2011/12 the need to buy an annuity by age 75 moves to age 77) – which is taxable – or for the full pension fund to be used to buy pension benefits.

If you are a member of an occupational final salary pension scheme, then the size of the tax-free cash and the amount of the pension payable depends on the number of years service with your employer and the actuarial factors employed within the scheme rules such as final salary definitions, as well as additional funding to boost benefits such as AVCs or free-standing AVCs, as well as stakeholder pension benefits, for employed earners. You can contribute to both an employer scheme and your own personal pension scheme at the same time.

If you are a member of a defined contribution scheme, then the end benefits are not exactly known and are dependent on funding requirements – again actuarially determined. An occupational defined contribution scheme, such as a money purchase group scheme is one such scheme. Group and individual personal pension schemes are others. There is a great variety of these occupational schemes – personal pension plans (PPPs), self-invested personal pensions (SIPPs) for the self employed; SSAS, small self-administered schemes; Executive Personal Pension schemes (EPPs) are examples.

A combination of pension funds plus an investment and savings portfolio, as well as property investments and other diversified investments would form the basis for a retirement plan.

There is no question that for most people, pension funding will form the bulk of their retirement planning portfolios. Proper structuring and asset allocation using available disposable income needs to be done, taking into account risk assessment and the types of investments best suited to your risk profile.

Your age is important, as is the number of years of work or employment left to accumulate wealth and then to manage it effectively. Protecting your assets and wealth is equally important. If you become disabled or die, or if a spouse does, then your plans need to be protected. It makes common sense to protect pension payments, and to limit the risks associated with wealth loss.

You may do a tremendous job in building up your retirement portfolio, but at retirement, making decisions can be crucial. The right decisions can significantly increase your income, improve your wealth and protect your position; the wrong ones can mean less income, or wasting wealth.

Retirement Countdown Planning should begin at least 10 years before retirement date. It becomes more urgent as the retirement date looms, and different actions are required at the various stages. For example, a 55-year old retiring at age 60 would like to see more cash going into pension funding and possibly a scaling down of other less important employee benefits. Up to two years from retirement, you would want to be eliminating debt, making sure the mortgage is paid off and buying new white goods for your house.

With the introduction of stakeholder pensions, the pensions environment changed. Children can begin pension plans (or have it begun for the child by a parent or grandparent), and those without relevant earnings can also have a pension scheme, contributing up to £3,600 gross (£2,880 net). Tax reliefs on contributions immediately increase the return of the investment.

Retirement planning is not only about building investments and pension plans for your old age. It is also about setting objectives, and doing other things, such as tax planning, estate planning, planning with tax-free lump sums, working closely with employers and the best use of employee benefits for wealth creation.

Pensions Simplified is an essential part of the retirement planning mix.

3

Different Types of Pension Fund

A Day (6th April 2006) brought together all pension schemes under one regime, subject to the same rules. However, there are many different types of pension fund, each with its own set of pension fund rules. These will remain in existence and investors will still have choice as to which schemes to enter into; and may enter into more than one pension scheme if it suits them. Contributions to any pension scheme are subject to overall funding limits on contributions and the size of pension fund, and these limits increase over time. Contrary to what people may believe, these different pension schemes are not merely amalgamated into one scheme. They remain as separate pension schemes, subject to that particular pension scheme's rules.

Other than the state pension schemes, broadly speaking, there are two main differences in pension funds. Every other variation springs from these two types. Pension funds can be divided into either **defined benefit** (DB) pension schemes or **defined contribution** (DC) pension schemes.

Defined benefit pension schemes (DB) *(final salary schemes)*

This type of scheme is best typified by what is known as the final salary scheme. Defined benefit because the recipient knows exactly how much his or her pension fund will be, based on a pre-determined formula. The unknown fact is how much funding is required to make the defined benefit a reality. This is an actuarial calculation based on factors such as age, length of time to go to retirement, the amount of money currently in the fund, interest rates and investment returns as well as other factors.

Nowadays, very few new final salary schemes are being taken out by businesses for their employees. The reasons are numerous, but in the main, the very high cost of funding required by the employer to maintain final salary scheme benefits, and the new accounting provision for defined benefit schemes in the balance sheets of companies (where, if the scheme is under-funded, it can reduce profits of the company).

However, most large companies have a final salary scheme for their employees, as does the Government for its employees, and this type of scheme is undoubtedly one of the best forms of pension provision. A recent trend is to move from a defined benefit scheme to a defined contribution scheme, and many employers have taken this route to reduce future pension funding costs. Recently the Government has established the Protected Pension Fund (PPF) to assist member employees where their pension funds are at risk where the employer has become insolvent, and is a defined benefit scheme only.

The defined benefit pension scheme allows both employer and employee to contribute to it. The employee can contribute an extra amount to boost eventual retirement benefits through what is known as the AVC, or additional voluntary contribution scheme. The AVC is with the main scheme provider to the employer. Alternatively, the employee can contribute to a product provider of his or her choice – this is known as a free-standing AVC, or FSAVC. In recent times, the stakeholder pension contract is being used more for AVC type contributions, as a cheaper alternative.

Normal retirement age

If the scheme was approved before the 25th July 1991, then retirement ages usually fall between the ages of 60 and 70 for men and 55 and 70 for women. However, if a woman is at least a 20% director, then the retirement age minimum is age 60. For schemes set up after the 25th July 1991, the age range is 60 to 75 for all members.

You can retire early (from age 50), but with reduced pension benefits, or later than the retirement age of the fund with increased benefits, but subject to a maximum of 2/3 of final remuneration. If not a 20% director and you have over 40 years service, you may qualify for a pension of up to 75% of final remuneration on actual retirement after the normal retirement date. Many pension contracts are being re-written to account for age discrimination and to allow for greater flexibility in retirement, after A Day on 6th April 2006.

There is no longer any special treatment based on occupation after A Day. Professional footballers and ballerinas could retire from their schemes at age 35, cricketers and trapeze artists at 40 – and they still can, if they had a pension fund before A Day. People taking up pension funds after A Day lose these valuable early-retirement concessions, and will have to wait until age 55.

Defined contribution pension scheme (DC) *(money purchase)*

This type of pension scheme is based on a pre-determined level of contributions to make up the pension fund or pension scheme (as opposed to a defined benefit pension scheme, where the contribution levels are largely unknown from year to year, and actuarially determined). Contributions may be set for employer-sponsored defined contribution schemes where, for example, the employer pays 6% of salary and the employee pays 3%; or may vary, for example, if an individual is self-employed and makes contributions based on HMRC limits each year.

At the end of the day, you get what you pay for under a defined contribution scheme. The value of the pension scheme itself depends on the contributions made and how well they are invested, the costs of the scheme, and other factors.

At retirement, the value of the pension fund can be apportioned for tax-free cash and a reduced pension, or no tax-free cash and a higher pension. The way in which pensions are paid also differs from a defined benefit scheme. A defined contribution scheme pays a pension through purchasing an annuity for the individual at retirement date. A defined benefit scheme, like a final salary scheme, may also use annuities to buy the pension, but are not restricted to this route – pensions could be paid from the fund itself, from the sale of assets, or even out of employer's cash flow.

There are different types of defined contribution pension schemes available, each type having its own set of rules and limitations. Most schemes are approved by HMRC, but some may be unapproved (like a FURBS or EFRBS).

The most common types of defined contribution pension schemes are given below, as well as their uses.

Personal Pension Plan Scheme (PPP)

Largely used by the self-employed. Employees without employer pension schemes may contribute (or the employer may do so) to a personal pension plan. You must have net relevant earnings to qualify after the first £3,600, and contributions are based on taxable income at up to 100% of relevant earnings at up to £255,000 in 2010/11 or £3,600, whichever is the greater. Minimum age 18. Can retire after age 55 and before age 75 (From 2011/12 the need to buy an annuity by age 75 moves to age 77).

Self-invested Personal Pension Plan (SIPP)

A personal pension plan where the individual decides how and where the contributions are to be invested. They are cheap to set up. However, most SIPP providers expect large annual contributions. A wide range of investment possibilities includes investing in residential and commercial properties (but not residential properties unless part of a portfolio – strict rules apply), traded endowment policies and other choices. Contributions are as for the personal pension regime, and retirement ages.

Stakeholder Pension Plan (SPP)

Based on a Personal Pension Plan, but with a lower-costed charging structure, it has other benefits such as cat-marked standards. Used by the self-employed, employees where there is no employer pension fund availability, or employees who are on an employer's pension fund. (Before A Day, the employee had to earn less than £30,000 per annum. After A Day (5th April 2006) the previous restrictions fall away as to earnings and the employee can have more than one pension fund and contribute up to the annual allowance). Minimum entry age is at birth. Retirement age is from 55 to 75. From 2011/12 the need to buy an annuity by age 75 moves to age 77.

You do not require taxable earnings, and can contribute up to £3,600 gross a year. Anyone can have a stakeholder pension plan, including children. The contribution is made net of basic rate tax (£2,880).

Group Personal Pension Plans (GPPP)

A Group Personal Pension Plan is one where an employer sets up a number of Personal Pension Plans for employees within a group arrangement to achieve economies of scale and cheaper pension administration costs. Each individual employee has a personal pension plan account within the group arrangement. Usually the employer contributes as well as the employee. If employer contributions are 3% or more, then this satisfies the stakeholder pension equivalent for employers. There can be flexibility within the grouping for individual retirement arrangements. A GPPP can be used to contract out of S2P, when the scheme is known as an appropriate personal pension scheme (APPS).

The maximum age to contribute to is age 74 (this may change as the retirement age changed in the 2010 Emergency Budget), but the final retirement age is 75, now and age 77 from 2011/12. Premiums paid can achieve tax relief at your highest marginal rate of tax as an employee, whilst the employer making contributions has them allowed against corporation tax. NI contributions can also be avoided through making contributions. The fund grows free of all taxes and part of the fund can be taken tax-free at retirement. Widows and widowers qualify for pension benefits, and on death, benefits under trust avoid tax. GPPPs fall under the personal pension scheme rules, not the rules of an occupational pension fund. They also allow employers to avoid most of the requirements of the Pensions Act 1995.

The new 'defined contribution regime' is an attempt by the Government to merge the stakeholder and personal pension regimes. From October 2001, employers with more than 4 employees must offer access to a designated stakeholder pension scheme. Currently over 70,000 employers are in default of this provision, and there has only been one prosecution to date. Employers are exempt if a GPPP is offered, but only if it makes a contribution of at least 3% of basic pay, and other conditions.

From 2012 the stakeholder scheme will be largely superseded by the new compulsory personal pension account for all employees, no matter the size of the business. This is called NEST – National Employment Savings Trust.

Salary Sacrifice

The employer contribution is often funded through 'salary sacrifice'. The employee decides on a net figure to contribute, and the employer adds to this net contribution the savings in tax made by the employee, as well as National Insurance contributions savings made by both the employer and the employee. The full contribution is made by the employer and the employee cannot deduct any tax or expand their basic rate tax band. However, the new gross contribution is better by 20-30% than if the employee merely made the contribution and claimed the tax back for the contribution made.

Salary sacrifice is an attractive way for an employer to use the tax system to increase pension funding for an employee at no extra cost.

Examples

Employee A
Salary	£50,000
Employee net contribution	£234 per month (£2,808 pa)
Salary after sacrifice	£47,192
Gross Employee Contribution	£355.68 made up of
Equivalent Net Contribution	£234
Tax Saving Employee	£93.60
Employee NI savings	£28.08
+	
Employer NI Savings	£29.95
=	
Total Pension Contribution	£385.63 per month
Plus ER contribution at %	£0
Total pension contribution	**£385.63 per month**

Conclusion: if you are a higher rate taxpayer making a net contribution of £234 per month (£2,808 per year) without employer additions, HMRC would have added back £58.50 (£702 p.a.) to make £3,510 p.a. (£292.50 p.m.) going into your pension plan. You will also get another 20% tax relief on your contribution of £561.60 p.a. (£46.80) as a higher rate taxpayer. Pension contribution plus additional tax relief is £339.30 per month.

If you make a salary sacrifice of the pension payment you pay tax on the reduced salary. The tax savings and NI savings are added to your contribution. As the employer makes the contribution on your behalf, you do *not* get the HMRC uplift of 20%. With salary sacrifice and the employer making the contribution, the total pension contribution is £385.63. You are therefore £46.33 p.m. better off through the salary sacrifice route. The employer gets a tax deduction on the full £385.63 p.m. as it makes the contribution.

Employee B

Salary	£25,000
Employee net contribution	£100 per month (£1,200 pa)
Salary after sacrifice	£23,800
Gross Employee Contribution	£131 made up of
Equivalent Net Contribution	£100
Tax Saving Employee	£20
Employee NI savings	£11
+	
Employer NI Savings	£12.80
=	
Total Pension Contribution	£143.80 per month
Plus ER contribution at %	£0
Total pension contribution	**£143.80 per month**

Conclusion: if you are a basic rate payer making a contribution of £100 per month without employer additions, HMRC would have added back £25 (20%) to make £125 p.m. going into your pension plan. You are therefore £18.80 p.m. better off through salary sacrifice. The employer gets a tax deduction on the full £143.80 p.m. as it makes the contribution.

Under the 'salary sacrifice' method, the employee foregoes the related salary portion and the employer contributes the **gross** salary plus the employer NI saved to the pension. Note that salary sacrifice may affect your other benefits, such as group life (as based on salary), and also incapacity and redundancy benefits. Group scheme providers can still give 'gross' benefits (as opposed to after salary sacrifice benefits) if required.

Under the new restrictive rules on contributions for high earners, the amount of salary sacrificed will be added back to your income if used for pension benefits and you earn £130,000 or more per year. However, salary sacrifice for earners below that level can use this methodology to reduce their taxable earnings to below the level where personal allowances are lost – at £100,000 in 2010/2011. That way they save the personal allowance and have an uplift to their pension fund.

Retirement Annuity (RA)

Although not offered since 1988, individuals may have existing RA plans. If so, they can still contribute to these plans, and could previously make carry forward and carry back pension contributions, but this is no longer available from April 6th 2006 (personal pension plans lost the ability to carry forward contributions after 6th April 2001). Contributions are based on net relevant earnings and are now within the overall limits of 100% of salary or taxable earnings up to £255,000 in 2010/11 or £3,600 gross (£2,880 net) if no earnings. Retirement ages are from 60 to 75. Retirement annuities were mainly for the self-employed, and the contribution basis is now the same as for any other pension scheme.

Executive Pension Plan (EPP)

This is an occupational pension scheme for an executive, or a spouse, for example, employed in the business. An EPP has an accelerated funding programme depending on the member's age, sex and years to retirement. Retirement dates are between ages 55 and 75.

Small Self-Administered Pension Scheme (SSAS)

An occupational pension scheme that has fewer than 12 members (i.e. no more than 11 members). With the same retirement range as EPPs of 55 to 75 (uplifted to 77 in 2010), the SSAS is mainly for company controlling directors, partners, or selected senior employees. Special rules restrict contribution levels by directors, as well as the types of investments undertaken. However, the SSAS can invest in commercial property, take out mortgages, buy shares in a private company (as well as the sponsoring company). Pension benefits are calculated as for occupational pension schemes.

Money Purchase Pension Schemes (MP)

MPs are occupational pension schemes, with defined contributions.

Defined Contribution schemes (DC)

The new defined contribution regime for pensions has merged personal pensions and stakeholder pensions together with money purchase occupational pension funds that opt in.

All of the above types of pension scheme depend on contributions being made and invested to provide a pension and tax-free cash.

The amount of tax-free cash and pensions or annuities payable depends on the type of pension fund arrangement. Occupational pension schemes have different rules and formulae to schemes for the self-employed, for example. After A Day, 6th April 2006, there is now one single pension's regime. If you did not ring-fence your tax-free cash and fund value on existing schemes before A Day (or during the transitional period to 2009) then all schemes offer 25% of the fund value as tax-free cash.

Additional Voluntary Contributions (AVC)

An AVC pension scheme is one where additional voluntary contributions are paid to an occupational pension scheme in addition to normal contributions, to obtain extra pension benefits. Funds saved in this way boost the retirement pension from the main scheme. Up to 15% of salary (including the value of taxable benefits, such as a company car) may previously be contributed to an AVC scheme (before A Day). After A Day, up to 100% of salary to £255,000 may be contributed in total to any number of schemes in 2010/11.

Free-Standing AVCs (FSAVC)

Employees may make additional voluntary contributions into a money purchase fund of their choice, within HMRC limits. This means they can make their contributions to a product provider that does not provide the main pension scheme benefits.

FURBS or EFRBS (Employer Funded Retirement Benefit Scheme)

A FURBS is a Funded Unapproved Retirement Benefit Scheme, in trust, used as a top-up to other pension schemes, and usually when the other pension scheme was at the old regime's pensions cap and could accept no further contributions, or where there was no other pension scheme and the employee requires a fund consisting of a tax-free lump sum cash payment, rather than a pension which is taxable. The contributions made are tax deductible to the employer, but taxable in the hands of the employee and national insurance contributions are payable. The fund itself is taxed at rates below the maximum personal income tax rate, and the proceeds are tax-free on FURBS existing prior to A Day. After A Day there are no tax advantages. FURBS are now called 'employer financed retirement benefit schemes'. Unapproved benefits accrued after A Day will be taxable on the member and only 25% may be taken as a cash lump sum. Contributions to an existing FURBS after A Day will have the fund apportioned to that before (tax-free) and after A Day (taxable). Pre A Day, funds will be inheritance tax-free on death – after A Day, funds will not be inheritance tax exempt.

Some people may have had an UURBS – an unfunded unapproved retirement benefit scheme – it had the same structure as a FURB, but was not funded, with a lump sum being payable to the executive. There was a window of opportunity within three months of A Day to roll this into a registered scheme and not have it count towards the annual allowance.

Other pension schemes

Other pension schemes would include those used to transfer pensions from one scheme to another. For example, a Section 32 Buyout Bond can receive pension transfers. There is also the Individual Pension Account (IPA), which introduces the concept of a pooled pensions investment for savings. The idea is to give one control over a pension savings vehicle, investing in gilts, collective investments and quoted shares, and is similar to the American 401k pensions savings plan.

A Day has also introduced the concept of the Alternatively Secured Pension (ASP) and the unsecured pension. These relate to drawdown from a pension fund account after age 75 (From 2011/12 the need to buy an annuity by age 75 moves to age 77) for the ASP instead of buying an annuity; and before age 75 (from 2011/12 age 77) for the Unsecured Pension, and are covered in the section on annuities and drawdown.

Protected rights

The pension fund portion of rebated national Insurance contributions from employees and employers is known as 'protected rights'. Previously you could only retire from the protected rights fund at the age of 60 and there was no tax-free cash allowable. Now you can retire from the age of 55 (if the protected rights portion is not in an occupational scheme), and take 25% in tax-free cash. Protected rights must still provide for a pension for dependents.

Electronic filing

Those not electronically filing their pension scheme returns after 16th October 2007 may face a penalty.

4

Pensions Simplification – The New Rules and Overview

The main changes introduced by A Day, after 6th April 2006, are on how much can be saved towards pension funding, the maximum amount of pension fund allowed and how and when benefits may be taken. There are also transitional arrangements for existing funds and protecting benefits that may exceed the new limits.

All UK approved and unapproved schemes have been affected. Individuals can belong to different schemes at the same time, and draw a pension whilst still working.

Standard Lifetime Allowance – SLA

The value of benefits from all pension arrangements is tested against the SLA. If you go over the allowance, a tax penalty will apply – the lifetime allowance charge. At A-Day the SLA was £1.5 million. It is scheduled to increase each year and is given as follows:

2008/09 £1.65 million
2009/10 £1.75 million
2010/11 £1.8 million (frozen at this level to 2015/16)

The lifetime allowance is reviewed every five years, and is expected to rise broadly in line with prices. For defined benefit schemes, this equates to the deemed capital value of accrued rights. This is achieved by multiplying the accrued pension entitlement by a factor of 20. If your annual pension is to be say £20,000 then the underlying fund value is £20,000 x 20 – £400,000.

If there is a pension in payment at A Day, a factor of 25 is used to value it against the standard lifetime allowance. For example, if your employer pension fund is paying you £20,000 p.a. as a pension, then the underlying fund is valued at £20,000 x 25 = £500,000. This is relevant if you have another pension fund accruing fund benefits after A Day, for the purposes of the SLA.

The penalty for funds accrued above the SLA is as follows (recovery tax charges):

- 25% where excess funds are taken as income
- 55% where excess funds are taken as a lump sum

Pension term assurance and death in service benefits payments can affect the SLA and be grouped together with pension funds and tested against the SLA. These death funds must be taken into account when assessing how much can be funded for.

Example

> John has a pension term life policy for £350,000 payable if he dies before age 65. In 2009/10 the balance of his lifetime allowance is £1.75 million – £350,000 = £1,400,000 available for pension funding. However, in 2010/11 the gap has increased to £1,450,000 as the SLA will have increased to £1.8 million, allowing for additional pension funding and life cover if required.

A pension credit acquired from a divorce settlement prior to A Day may have been registered with HMRC within 3 years of A day to increase an individual's personal lifetime allowance to take account of the pension credit.

Protecting existing pension funds and tax-free cash

If you had a pension fund close to or over the SLA at A Day (6th April 2006), then you are able to protect your accumulated funds and future tax-free cash lump sums through applying for 'protection'. You can have either Primary Protection or Enhanced Protection or both, and must have registered for it by 5th April 2009.

Primary Protection

Primary Protection is available for those with accrued funds and pension entitlements in excess of the SLA (£1.5 million) at A Day. Here the pre-A Day fund(s) value becomes your Personal Lifetime Allowance (PLA), and is indexed in line with the SLA up to the date when your benefits are crystallised. This means your funds will be not be subject to the recovery charge tax for being over the SLA. Tax-free cash entitlements and the fund value is protected.

Enhanced Protection

Enhanced protection is for you if you do not intend to make any further contributions after A Day. In other words, you opt out of active membership of your pension scheme(s). If so, then all benefits payable after A Day will usually be exempt from the recovery charge. You will enjoy the benefit of fund growth until you take your pension benefits.

43

If you register for both protections, you could then opt out of enhanced protection and continue to make pension contributions, whilst still benefiting from primary protection.

The member must apply for primary and enhanced protection to secure a higher level of benefits within the lifetime allowance limits. This application could have been made up to 5th April 2009 on HMRC form APSS 200 – you can only have enhanced protection if no further pension contributions were made (and no further benefit accrual has occurred) after 6th April 2006.

Annual allowance – maximum pension contributions

Annual tax relief on personal contributions is the higher of £3,600 and 100% of UK earnings subject to an annual allowance. The annual allowance excludes protected rights contributions.

The annual allowance is as follows, and rises by £10,000 per annum:

2008/09	£235,000
2009/10	£245,000
2010/2011	£255,000 (frozen at this level to 2015/16)

For details of the £20,000 special annual allowance for earners of £150,000 or more, see the section at the end of this chapter.

There is no limit on employer contributions. Employers can make up the difference between an individual's contributions to all schemes and the Annual Allowance. However, any contributions paid by or on behalf of an individual that exceed the Annual Allowance in any one tax year will be subject to a tax charge of 40%, payable by the individual (as this is seen as a taxable benefit in kind). If contributions are to a defined benefit scheme (final salary scheme), then the value inflow is tested against the Annual Allowance. The 'contribution' is tested by multiplying the increase in accrued entitlement over the year by a factor of 10.

Under the new restrictive contributions test for high earners, the method of valuation of the underlying pension scheme will change. There may well be problems with valuations going forward as all schemes need to give affected members information about their pension. The value of benefits will have to be calculated using by using age related factors based on age and normal pension age. Defined benefit schemes are affected, and the age related factors will apply instead of the 10:1 factors that have been used since A day, to measure the annual increase in benefit value for the purposes of the annual allowance. Older people may face a higher tax bill than if simple factors had been used. Defined benefit schemes will become more complicated for trustees, employers and providers. Schemes and benefit provision will no doubt be reviewed by employers as costs will go up.

Comparing the new regime to the previous one

Contributions to personal pension plans and retirement annuities are no longer calculated as a factor of age to amount, e.g. at age 30 you could have contributed 17.5% of taxable income in the past. Your contribution was also subject to the pensions cap on contributions. This has also been abolished under the new regime.

Example

Assume Roger is age 45 and earns a salary of £200,000 p.a.

Under the old regime, he could have contributed 20% x £200,000 = £40,000 to a personal pension plan in 2005/06, limited to the earnings cap of £105,600, which is an actual contribution of £21,120 which is tax relievable. Under the *old regime*, Roger can contribute the full £200,000 as 100% of salary to his pension funding, and have it tax relievable as being within the Annual Allowance of £245,000 for 2009/10 — very generous indeed. As a 40% taxpayer, relief is at his highest rate of tax for that portion above the basic rate tax band. *However*, under the 2009 Budget proposals, confirmed in 2010, unless Roger was making regular contributions, as his income is over £150,000, he may be subject to the Special Annual Allowance rules of £20,000 - £30,000 contributions p.a.

From A Day, 6th April 2006, carry back and carry forward of tax relief will no longer be allowed under any type of pension arrangement.

Employee contributions

Employees on occupational pension schemes could previously contribute 15% of taxable earnings to an AVC/FSAVC or personal pension plan under the old rules. The employee had to have earnings under £30,000 per annum. This prohibition has also been swept away and employees can contribute to all schemes within the limit of their £255,000 Annual Allowances.

Employer tax relief

Employer contributions are tax relievable, but larger premiums may need to be spread over a number of years. Employers' contributions are usually allowed as a deduction in the period in which they are paid. If pension contributions have increased by more than 210% from a previous to the present accounting period, and the excess amount is £500,000 or more, the contributions are spread over 2-4 years for deduction purposes.

Spreading of tax relief for pension contributions (PBR13)

New legislation was introduced in the *Finance Act 2008* to ensure that the rules that spread tax relief for large employer contributions relative to their contribution in the previous year cannot be circumvented (from 10th October 2007). You cannot avoid spreading of contributions by routing them through a new company. Pension contributions are tax relievable against profits (deductible to the employer company). Large contributions are spread by up to 4 years (where it is more than 210% of the contribution paid in the previous chargeable period, and exceeds 110% of the contribution paid in that previous period by at least £500,000).

Contributions made net of basic rate tax

Pension contributions made by individuals are made net of basic rate tax at 20% in 2010/11. If a higher rate taxpayer, the balance is claimed through the tax return at 20%. There is also an opportunity for a non-taxpayer to have HMRC contribute to his or her pension plans as pension contributions are made net of basic rate tax and HMRC pays the 20% to the pensions provider. If a 40% taxpayer and contributing £3,600 to a personal pension plan, the amount paid will be £2,880, net of basic rate tax. You then claim a further 20% x £3,600 = £720 through your tax return. (Note that you get higher rate tax relief on your gross contribution, not the net contribution). You therefore invest £2,880 and HMRC invests £720 + tax relief returned as a higher rated taxpayer of £720 = £1,440. Not a bad deal if you can get it!'

In specie contributions

You do not have to make a cash pension contribution either. It is allowable to make an 'in specie' transfer to a pension scheme of an approved asset (such as a commercial property), where the value of the property is transferred to the pension fund as a pension contribution. The value goes in net of basic rate tax and you claim the balance up to your highest rate. You may have to do this over more than one tax year if the value is greater than 100% of your earnings or above the Annual Allowance. You may have capital gains tax to pay and SDLT (stamp duty) if transferring your own asset into the pension fund – which you may now do.

Family or third party contributions

A grandparent can make a pension contribution for a grandchild, or in fact for anyone – they do not need to be related – for the £3,600 gross (£2,880 net). The scheme member would get the tax relief on contributions.

Pension caps

There is now no cap as a percentage of earnings and no 'earnings cap'. Pension contributions are made within the overall contribution allowance of 100% or salary up to £255,000 per annum.

Annual Allowance not applying

The Annual Allowance will not apply in the year pension benefits are taken in full, or the year in which the member dies. One can therefore make a 'final' payment into a pension fund that ignores the Annual Allowance, but the value of the pension fund must still fall within the Lifetime Allowance (SLA).

High earners

The changes announced in the 2009 Budget are far-reaching, and affect those earning £150,000 and over from the 2009/10 tax year, and/or the two previous tax years. Whilst there may be changes or variations going forward, the following is the position to date. (See also HMRC Budget 2009 BN47 'Limiting Tax relief for High Income Individuals (anti-forestalling) and HMRC Pensions: 'Limiting Tax relief for High Income Individuals – Guidance for Individuals 22 April 2009' for a full explanation. There is also a Guide for the Pensions Industry. www.hmrc.gov.uk/budget2009/ is the website address. The pension schemes helpline is on 0845 600 2622.)

From 6th April 2009:

- If earning £149,999 p.a. or less : no change, and the usual rules apply, and you get full tax relief.
- If earning more than £150,000 (all income) and you have been making regular contributions (at least quarterly), and do not change your normal pattern of regular contributions, nor those of your employer contributions, and you do not increase your pension contributions after 22nd April 2009, then these rules do not apply to you.
- If earning more than £150,000 (all income) and you make annual contributions of less than £20,000, then the new rules do not apply to you.
- If earning £150,000 or more in 2009/10 or the previous two tax years (2007/08 and 2008/09) – you will be deemed to be in the new restrictive category if in 2009/10 you do not earn over £150,000, but you did in any of the past two years, and the new rules apply to you.
- There is a special annual allowance applying of £20,000 in any one tax year and tax relief will be given at the basic rate, not the higher rate of tax, above this level, if pension contributions exceed this limit and are not within the exemptions.

- If your pension contributions in any one year are greater than £20,000 then you need to do the income headroom check for the past two tax years to establish that the limits are not exceeded. You may have regular contributions of say £2,000 per month (£24,000 p.a.) and a single premium contribution of £50,000. Whilst the regular premium contributions will be within the rules, the single premium will be subject to the special annual allowance charge. This is so, even if you make it regularly, i.e. annually, as it is not within the definition of regular which is at least quarterly.

- 'Relevant income' is important. This is your total income before pension contributions, personal allowances and other reliefs and deductions. You can then deduct normal deductions for reliefs, including trading losses, and including pension contributions – but up to a maximum of £20,000, and also deduct gift aid contributions. You must add back any salary sacrifice in return for pension contributions (presumably though not for other benefits). Deductions could take your £150,000+ income to below that level.

- Whilst pension contributions made by an employer are deductible to the employer, they could be taxable on the employee (if going over the £20,000 p.a.).

- Any normal, ongoing and regular pension savings are known as 'protected inputs', and increases in pension funding due to promotion and salary increases could also be protected inputs. This is also the case for contracted increases in a scheme before 22nd April 2009.

- The special allowance charge is really aimed at those earning over £150,000 who increase their pension contributions to total more than £20,000 in any one tax year, above the protected pension input amount.

- If you do not know what your income will be in the tax year (many people do not), then if you have a relevant income of £150,000 or more in 2009/10 and 2010/11 or either of the previous two tax years, and you increased the rate of pension savings on or after 22nd April 2009, then you could be affected. If your income is below this or you do not increase your pension savings, you will not be affected.

- The special annual allowance will run alongside the existing annual allowance. If you exceed both allowances, then the special annual allowance charge will be reduced by the excess over the annual allowance (to avoid a double tax charge). The tax rate for excess pension savings for 2009/10 is 20%.

- There are a number of rules and guidelines affecting occupational schemes. For example, if you leave your current employer, and start your own personal pension scheme, the new scheme will not count as a protected pension input. Entering into a new arrangement to buy back years service after 22nd April 2009 will be a non-protected pension input.

- The pension input period for the special annual allowance will always be the tax year. It is not the same as for the annual allowance as that would allow individuals to have three input periods covering two tax years, with an additional £20,000, which would not be allowable.
- The one mitigation for those earning over £150,000 is that they should at least put in the £20,000 for the next tax year. From 6th April 2010 they should be able to *claim 50%* tax relief on their pension contributions for 12 months – the new tax rate of 50% comes in 2010/11, but the new rules on lowering tax relief do not come in until the 2011/12 tax year.

The Treasury is expecting to rake in around £7 billion a year from the new tax rates, the reduction in pension reliefs, and the increase in NI for individuals from 11% to 11.5% announced in the pre-budget report. The removal of the personal allowance for those earning between £100,000 and £112,950 (zero from this latter figure, going forward) from April 2010, means an effective tax rate of 60%. Reducing a salary to below £100,000 will cut that rate of tax back to 40%. Investors will be considering salary sacrifice, making use of tax efficient investments like ISAs and EIS qualifying investments, transferring investments to a lower taxed spouse, and setting up a limited company (where corporation tax rates are 21% to 28%), to make savings.

The latest

In the 2010 Budgets there is confirmation of previous budgets that from 2011/12 tax relief on pension contributions for individuals with income over £150,000 will be gradually tapered. At £180,000 you will only receive basic rate relief (20%) on contributions. Total income is before deduction for pension contributions and charitable donations. If your income is £130,000 and over and together with your employer pension contributions takes you to £150,000 or over, your pension tax reliefs will be tapered. Anti-forestalling measures came into effect for 2009/10 and 2010/11 to prevent pension contribution increases before the new rules came into effect. The special annual allowance of £20,000 - £30,000 (depending on your circumstances) should cease to apply *after* the 2010/11 tax year (as the tapered pension relief rates come in then).

Contribution Levels 2010/11 and 2011/12

Income

Less than £3,600, eg non-earners, children, retired	£3,601 - £43,875	£43,875 - £129,999	£130,000+ in 2010/11	£150,000 - £180,000+ From 2011/12
⬇	⬇	⬇	⬇	⬇
Invest up to £3,600 at a cost of £2,880	Invest up to 100% of earnings with 20% added back by HMRC	Invest up to 100% of earnings, have 20% added back by HMRC and claim 20% (40% relief)	Invest at least £20,000, have the HMRC add back 20% and claim a further 20% (40% relief). Additional contributions over £20,000 get 20% relief.	Invest at least £20,000, relief to be tapered from 50% down to 20%

From 2011/2012, with income below £130,000 you do not have to determine the value of employer's contributions and continue to receive tax relief at your marginal rate; above that, the employer's contributions are added to your pre-tax income. If £150,000 or more, then tax relief restrictions apply, if not, full relief continues. Beware salary sacrificed may be added back into income, if done for greater pension benefits.

Examples of Taper Relief

Income	£150,000	£155,000	£160,000	£165,000	£170,000	£175,000	£180,000
Max. Rate of relief	50%	45%	40%	35%	30%	25%	20%

The relief is a decrease of £% for every £1,000 or part of gross income.

Example: If earnings plus employer contributions are £155,000, and a pension contribution of £25,000 is made. Relief is 40% on the first £20,000 and 50% on the remaining £5,000. However the maximum rate of taper relief is 45% at £155,000. As it is greater than 40% it only applies to contributions that would have received marginal rate relief of 50%. The contributions benefiting from the 40% rate of tax suffer no charge. There is therefore no tax charge on the first £20,000 of contribution, and a recovery charge of 5% is applied to the remaining 5% of contribution, i.e. £250.

Maximising Pension Contributions in 2010/11

Where anti-forestalling rules apply it is important to make contributions of up to £20,000 (or £30,000 if previously up to that level) in 2010/2011 to qualify for full higher rate tax relief. If relevant income is below £130,000, 2010/2011 is a good time to maximise pension contributions, as the limit could be reduced in the future.

Restoring the Personal Allowance

If caught by the effective rate of tax of 60% on income between £100,000 and £112,950 (through loss of the personal allowance of £6,475) should consider salary sacrifice and other income shifting strategies. Salary sacrifice could restore the personal allowance and reduce a 60% effective tax rate to say 40%. This becomes more important as National Insurance contributions increase by 1% from 6.4.20100, where employees with earnings above the UEL pay 2% and employers 13.8%.

Valuation of Pension Benefits

There may well be problems with valuations as all schemes need to give affected members information about their pension. The value of benefits will have to be calculated using by using age related factors based on age and normal pension age. Defined benefit schemes are affected, and the age related factors will apply instead of the 10:1 factors that have been used since A day, to measure the annual increase in benefit value for the purposes of the annual allowance. Older people may face a higher tax bill than if simple factors had been used. Defined benefit schemes will become more complicated for trustees, employers and providers. Schemes and benefit provision will no doubt be reviewed by employers as costs will go up.

5

Pensions for the Self-Employed and Those Who Are Not Members of the Employer's Pension Scheme

The self-employed are those working as sole traders, or essentially 'one man band' small companies, treated by HMRC as being self-employed. If self-employed, you could be working for yourself, or have employees working in your business. The general rule is that the self-employed are governed by the personal pension rules and may make pension contributions based on their 'net relevant earnings' to a personal pension plan (or to a retirement annuity account – although these were discontinued after 1988).

Those not members of the employer's pension scheme can also contribute to a personal pension plan on the basis as that outlined below for the self-employed.

The self-employed can also contribute to a stakeholder pension plan, especially in poor business years where they may not have sufficient income, and therefore no relevant earnings for normal pension contributions. Stakeholder pensions will take gross contributions of up to £3,600 (£2,880 net) without the need for net relevant earnings.

Contributions to HMRC approved pension schemes are tax allowable against taxable income, and contributions made reduce taxable income, and thereby tax payable.

The pension fund grows tax-free and at retirement date from 55 and age 75 (77 from 2011/12), can provide a tax-free lump sum and a reduced pension (annuity), or a higher pension without a tax-free lump sum. You can also take an income from your pension fund without having to retire, up to age 75 (77 from 2011/12), when you must take an alternatively secured pension (ASP) or an annuity. The choice is yours. Usually though, most people take the tax-free lump sum (now known as a pension commencement lump sum) as they feel they can control their own investments better, and may have uses for it beyond making investments, such as reducing mortgages or paying off debt.

Existing retirement annuity funds

If you have an existing retirement annuity fund, then continue with payments to this, as tax-free lump sums may be higher. You had until April 2009 to register for protection of your funds and higher tax-free cash (Primary or Enhanced Protection). You cannot carry-back nor carry-forward contributions anymore, as this allowance ended in the 2005/06 tax year. The normal retirement age is 60 (not 55 as with a personal pension plan); employers cannot make contributions to a retirement annuity, although after A Day, this may become a possibility (they can with a personal pension plan); and income draw-down is not possible through a retirement annuity (a transfer must first be made to a personal pension plan).

Older retirement annuity policies will only allow a refund of premiums plus, say, 4%-5% on death, although the life office can change this formula to a return of fund, if the right approaches are made. A return of fund will usually give a much higher refund.

The maximum contribution levels to a personal pension plan and to a retirement annuity, is100% of earnings with an Annual Allowance limit in 2010/11 of £255,000, or £3,600 gross if no earnings. Contributions to a retirement annuity are gross, whilst those to a personal pension plan are net of basic rate tax.

The type of pension plans that the self-employed can enjoy include regular premium contribution plans, for example £100 per month; or a single premium contribution of say £5,000 a year, or whenever. Single premiums are cheaper than regular premiums, as their costs are less.

Self-invested personal pension plans (SIPPs)

A SIPP is a personal pension plan, usually for high net worth individuals, partners and LLP members, who wish to self direct the investments of their pension planning.

SIPPs are useful to consolidate other pension plans into one plan. SIPPs can take transfers from other personal pension plans, retirement annuities, FSAVCs, executive pension plans (EPPs), other SIPPs, stakeholder pensions, paid up money purchase occupational pension schemes. Before transferring a pension scheme, check the exit penalties and charges, to see if this is worthwhile.

You can build up a pension fund which will grow tax-free. At retirement, 25% of the fund may be taken as tax-free cash and the balance can provide you with an income to age 75 (77 from 2011/12), when you must take an ASP (Alternatively Secured Pension) or an annuity. The income, pension or annuity is taxable.

Contributions

Contributions to the SIPP are made net of basic rate tax, and if a higher rate taxpayer, the balance of tax relief is claimed through your tax return. This is shown as follows:

Example

Dorothy wishes to contribute £10,000 to her SIPP, and is a higher rate taxpayer.
She pays £8,000 and HMRC pays £2,000 to make it up to £10,000. Dorothy can claim a further £2,000 (20%) through her tax return. So she ends up with a contribution of £10,000 which has cost her £6,000.
Dorothy can make contributions of up to the greater of £3,600 or 100% of salary or earnings up to £255,000 in the 2010/11 tax year. She can build a pension fund (including her other pension funds, if she has any) within her lifetime allowance of £1.8 million from 2010/11 to 2015/16.

Contributions need not be in money. You could make 'in specie' contributions of a property share for example, to your pension fund. These are made net of basic rate tax and higher rate taxpayers can make a reclaim for the difference between basic rate and higher tax rates.
To qualify for tax relief you must be aged under 75, and either resident in the UK at some time in the tax year, or have relevant UK earnings, or if overseas, be a Crown employee with general earnings subject to UK tax. You can be non-resident and get tax relief.
Earnings if salaried include the value of benefits in kind (taxable benefits); if self-employed the amount of profits you make (after adjustments for UK tax purposes).
Employer contributions are paid gross and can be paid in addition to your contributions, and are not part of your allowance. However, note that if the value of any benefits accrued in a final salary scheme along with total contributions to all other pensions exceed the Annual Allowance of £255,000 for 2010/11, then you would have to pay 40% tax on the excess.

Eligibility

If aged under 75 and resident in the UK. Includes children, non-earners, those already retired, members of occupational pension schemes (who were ineligible under the old rules).

54

Property purchase

The SIPP can invest in commercial property (not residential property), and can now purchase the property from a connected party. The SIPP can use its own funds, or make borrowings to do so.

A SIPP could borrow a maximum amount pre A Day of 75% of the purchase price of the property. Post A Day the maximum amount that can be borrowed is 50% of the current value of the scheme, less any outstanding loans.

If a property is to be purchased, then 100% of scheme assets plus any scheme borrowings can be used, making it 150% of the scheme's current value. Apart from property, borrowed money can be used for stocks and shares.

If for example, a scheme is currently valued at £700,000, then 50% of the value of the scheme is £350,000 that can be borrowed (before A Day it was much less usually as a percentage of the purchase price; pre-A Day will usually be less than 50% of the fund value). The rules are the same for SASSs. If a property is worth £200,000 then 75% is £150,000 (old rules) for borrowing; if the fund value is £1 million then 50% is £500,000, and that amount can be borrowed (new rules).

Buying the business premises could make sense. The rental income accruing is tax-free in the hands of the pension fund, and when the property is sold there is no capital gains tax payable, therefore all growth in the property is tax-free. The rental payments are deductible to the business for tax purposes.

Changes to the tax rules announced 15th April 2009 allow SIPPs and SSASs to restructure their borrowing terms on loans made against more than 50% of the fund's value without a tax penalty, so long as the amount borrowed is not increased. Leases on commercial property held by the pension scheme can also be re-negotiated allowing reduced rental to be paid, even where the property is let to connected members. Tax charges are also waived on loans where residential property is used as collateral.

Businesses borrowing funds from a SSAS could be doubling up on tax reliefs. The Government has boosted the annual investment allowance to £100,000 (from £50,000). The business borrows £100,000 from the SSAS and invests in plant and machinery. The business gets tax relief on repaying the loan to the pension scheme, as well as tax relief on investing in plant and machinery.

Lending money

A SIPP can lend money to any unconnected third party – individual or company. It cannot make a loan to a family member or the business where there are connected members. Up to 50% of the total net assets of the SIPP can be loaned. The loan must be for no longer than 5 years. The interest rate must be a minimum of 1% above base rate, and loaned monies must be repaid by equal instalments of interest and capital. The trustees make the loan, not the member.

Retirement flexibility

Income can be drawn down from the SIPP fund whilst still working from age 55. The balance of the fund remains invested to grow tax-free, rather than having to buy an annuity. At retirement, options include drawdown, phased retirement, and taking an annuity; not to mention 25% of the fund in tax-free cash.

Family SIPPs

Where members of a family or friends have a SIPP with the same provider, there were previously inheritance tax planning advantages. Any surplus under a member's SIPP on their death (after payment of death benefits) can be passed on to one or more SIPPs, which could be the SIPP of a grandchild or child. On the death of the member, the first obligation is to provide for a surviving spouse, civil partner or dependants; and surplus can be passed in this way, or on the second death.

If death occurs after taking benefits, or perhaps the tax-free lump sum, but before age 75 (77 from 2011/12), an income is first paid to any spouse, civil partner or financial dependant. Once the dependants are gone, the residual assets can pass to one or more family SIPPs. There would now be scheme sanction charges and IHT may be payable. See the chapter on IHT and pension funds.

If the member dies after age 75 (77 from 2011/12) , an income is first paid to financial dependants, spouse, civil partner, and when they pass on, the residual assets are added to the member's estate and inheritance tax is applied to the whole estate. If these pension assets fall within the nil rate band of £325,000 then no IHT is payable, and the SIPP assets could be passed to other family SIPPs (or indeed to other beneficiaries). Any amount above the nil rate band would be subject to IHT. However, as there is usually some passage of time between the first and second death, it may be that higher nil rate bands or even lower IHT rates exist at that time. Scheme sanction charges and penalties would apply to the residual funds, though.

A SIPP set up by a grandparent for a grandchild could be a useful way to pass on assets that would otherwise increase the grandparent's estate, to a pension fund for a grandchild, and also one to provide an income as opposed to a lump sum that may be squandered. Failure to provide for pension succession planning could end up with residual pension assets passing to a charity or the Duchy of Cornwall! Anything to make Prince Charles happier!

A SIPP can be topped up in the year of a member's death to reach the maximum pension fund limit of £1.8 million (2010/11). This provision overrides the Annual Allowance of £255,000. If a member had a fund of say £650,000, then his company could contribute a further £1,150,000 and have it tax relievable – albeit spread over a number of years. This may be advantageous for profit extraction to pass to family members through the family SIPP concept. Actually, you don't have to die to have the overriding provision for a final maximum contribution – this can occur in your year of retiring and taking benefits.

Family SIPPs can cost as low as £250 pa and started with a single contribution.

Investments

You can also have a Self-Invested Personal Pension Plan (SIPP), where you direct how the plan is to be invested. You have very wide investment options, from commercial property to investing into other pension fund investments. A SIPP's investment funds can be spread over a number of investment houses, and is more flexible at retirement, with regard to options.

Following A Day, the following are allowable SIPP and SSAS Investments:

Generally any investment is allowable unless restricted. Restricted investments are known as **taxable property**, which is residential property, whether in the UK or elsewhere, or **tangible moveable property**.

- **Taxable property** includes holiday houses and timeshare and certain hotels (other hotels may escape the restriction if the scheme owns the hotel but you never stay there) as well as beach huts. However, a residential home for children, an old age home, a hospital or hospice and a prison will fall outside of the definition for taxable property, as will students' halls of residence, but not flats or houses let to students. Be careful of mixed-use properties – they will usually be classed as residential, if they could be suitable for use as a dwelling.

- **Tangible moveable property** – things that can be touched and moved – includes investments where you may obtain a personal benefit, such as art, antiques, jewellery, fine wine, vintage cars, stamp collections, rare books, plant and machinery, office equipment etc. The Chancellor clamped down on residential properties and tangible moveable items being held as scheme investments when it was shown that possible abuse would happen, if allowed to continue. Tax charges apply if taxable property is acquired by the pension fund. These charges include an acquisition charge of 40%, a scheme sanction charge of 15% of value, a 15% unauthorised payments charge if the asset exceeds 25% of the scheme value. Income from the taxable property is taxed at 40%/50%, and if the asset is sold, capital gains tax is payable of 28%. Total penalties could therefore exceed 70%. The lesson to be learned from HMRC is stay well clear of restricted investments for pension funds. There is transitional protection for those schemes that have restricted investments as at 5th April 2006. The restrictions mentioned above only apply after 6th April 2006.

SIPP and SSAS investments may be made into almost anything else, including:

- commercial property you already own
- commercial property domestic and overseas
- collective investments, unit trusts, investment trusts, OEICs
- hedge funds, property funds
- residential properties only if through a UK Real Estate Investment Trust (REIT) and syndicates of at least 11 participants – no member can hold more than 10% of the syndicate (including associated persons)
- residential property for the use of an employee who is not a member of the pension scheme, nor connected with a scheme member, and required to occupy the property as a condition of employment, or the property is used in connection with business premises held as an investment of the scheme
- unquoted securities genuinely at arm's length from the member – but there is still clarity required on investing into your own company shares
- investment grade gold bullion
- indirect holdings of tangible moveable property where their market value is no greater than £6,000, and certain other conditions are met
- invest into commercial trading concerns, profession or vocation, where the pension scheme does not have control of the trading vehicle, there are no directors who are members of the pension scheme, no member will occupy or use the property, i.e. 'general diverse commercial vehicles' can be invested into
- stocks and shares – employer sponsored schemes can hold up to 5% of the fund value in shares of the employer or an associated company (There is no limit on the amount of shares to be held in other companies. Non employer-sponsored schemes can invest an unlimited amount of their assets in the shares of an employer or associated company, or any other company. However, there may be restrictions, such as investing into a company that owns a property (residential) and the scheme has a 100% of the shares.)
- traded life policies and traded endowment policies
- cash
- quoted stocks and shares
- insured funds
- trustee investment plans or bonds, National Savings
  … to name a few investment possibilities.

Investment planning and asset allocation are important aspects, as is the risk rating of the investor as well as the funds invested into.

HMRC can help you to save by giving generous tax reliefs to you. Contributions are paid net, putting pension contributions on a similar basis to the employed. All contributions are made net at 20%, the basic rate taxpayer's rate (even if only a 10% taxpayer). HMRC pays the difference to your pension fund. If a higher rate taxpayer, you claim the difference through your tax return or PAYE coding.

For example, if you are a 40% taxpayer, and wish to contribute £5,000 this year, you only pay (£5,000 – £1,000 (20%) = £4,000 and HMRC pays the rest into your fund to make up the £5,000. You can then also claim 20% x £5,000 = £1,000 back through your tax return (you receive this deduction on what you contribute gross). Your fund then grows tax-free and at retirement, 25% can come out tax-free as a lump sum. You could have had a total of 65% worth of tax reliefs through investing in pensions. It's probably one of the only times you will thank HMRC!

Getting your life assurance tax deductible – abolished in December 2006

From April 2006, it was possible to have pension term life assurance with tax deductible premiums. Premiums are paid net of basic rate tax at 20% and if a 40% taxpayer, an additional 20% is deductible from taxable income from 6th April 2008 for existing tax-deductible premiums pension term policies.

Unlike the previous regime where you had to have a pension to have deductible term assurance, under the new regime, to begin with you could have the deductible premiums without having a pension plan.

The pension term cover was available to age 75 and may be level, decreasing or increasing pension term. If waiver of premium benefits were required (where the life office pays the premium if you become sick, ill or disabled so that you cannot work, then the life office pays your pension term premium for you), these have to be supplied separately as the premium for waiver of premium cannot be tax relievable. Pension term pays out a lump sum tax-free on death within the pension term.

The amount of the sum assured should be added to your other pension fund benefits because it forms part of your lifetime allowance (SLA). Most life offices allow you to move to a non tax-relievable product should there be any danger of your exceeding your lifetime allowance limit. If, at death, the sum assured on a qualifying pension term policy when added to your other pension fund benefits, exceeds the lifetime allowance limit, then a recovery charge could arise at 55%. Funds are also aggregated with your death in service benefits in respect of the SLA. On death, if the policy is underwritten in trust, it should be free of inheritance taxes. Employer contributions to separate life assurance arrangements will not count towards the Annual Allowance for contributions, but individual premium payments for pension term life assurance will count towards the Annual Allowance which is £255,000 in 2010/11.

Life cover is important during the fund building stage. If your pension fund is not large enough to provide your dependants with a pension, then the life cover provides a tax-free lump sum that can be invested to provide for income. It is also important to cover liabilities, such as a mortgage and other debts and to provide for estate liquidity – to give much needed cash to an estate.

Whilst tax-deductible pension term policies are no longer available, life cover is still most important and should be considered, even if there is no tax relief. Some employer group life arrangements have deductible premiums and this should be considered if cost reduction is important.

Tax relief on existing PTA policies will be protected under the new rules in the *Finance Act 2007* and contributions to these policies will continue to receive tax relief. However, such policies cannot be varied to increase the benefits payable or extend the term of a policy – if any such adjustments are made, then the tax deduction benefits will cease. Tax relief on *employer* contributions are not affected by these changes, nor is tax relief on group life policies. The changes to tax relief on premiums only affect personal or individual pension term policies.

Example

> Penny requires £350,000 level term life cover to age 65. She can have conventional term cover where the premium is £37 per month, on average.

Your strategy would be to check your present coverages and consider life cover to protect your pension fund while it is building up. The life policy should be in trust and on death pays out a tax-free lump sum that can benefit your dependants.

Finance Act 2007 changes

Royal Assent for the *Finance Act 2007* was received on 19th July 2007. Provisions relating to pension schemes are in sections 68–70 and Schedules 18 to 20, where amendments are made to the *Finance Act 2004*. Section 68 and Schedule 18 remove the tax relief for personal term assurance for occupational schemes from 31st July 2007 and other pension schemes from 5th April 2007. Policies issued before the prescribed dates are protected for their existing tax reliefs. For occupational schemes this is 1st August 2007 (policy application received before 29th March 2007) and for other schemes it is 1st August 2007 where the application was received before 14th December 2006 (where there are no pension rights under the scheme) and 13th April 2007 where pension rights were being accrued. Varying the terms of a protected policy will lose the tax reliefs. Tax relief on employer contributions is not affected by these changes (group life schemes are therefore unaffected, and continue to enjoy tax relief on contributions).

6

Occupational Pension Schemes

– if in Work as an Employee or Director

An occupational pension scheme is another name for an employer-sponsored pension scheme. Occupational pension schemes will fall into three main categories:

(1) Defined Benefit Schemes (DBS)
(2) Defined Contribution Schemes (DCS) and
(3) AVCs and FSAVCs. Stakeholder pension schemes may now substitute for FSAVCs as a better deal.
(4) SSAS – Small self-administered pension schemes

We also have a 'defined contribution regime', not to be confused with an occupational pension scheme with defined contributions.

1. Defined benefit schemes

A defined benefit pension scheme is best described as an HMRC approved and exempt pension scheme, designed to pay out a defined benefit at retirement date, or earlier or later than the normal retirement date. These are usually final salary or average final salary pension schemes, based on final remuneration and years of service.

A move from one employer to another may mean a lower pension benefit, even if both offer a final salary pension scheme. If the former employer had a final salary defined benefit pension scheme, you may have to make that previous pension scheme 'paid up' and not transfer the benefit, as a pension would be based on your years' service in that pension scheme together with the years of service in your employer's new final salary pension scheme at your usual retirement age. However, if the new employer's pension scheme is different from the former employer's pension scheme, for example, you are moving from a defined contribution scheme (money purchase) to a defined benefit scheme (final salary), then it may be to your advantage to pay into your new employer's defined benefit scheme to buy what is called 'back service'.

That is if the rules allow it to be done.

As the defined benefit pension scheme is based on years' service, the less the years' service, the less the end pension benefit will be. An actuarial calculation may say that you can buy back 5 years of service for £50,000.

You have £50,000 in your previous employer's pension fund, and make the transfer. You then work for your new employer for, say, 15 years, but the back-service purchased gives you 20 years service with the new employer for the pensions formula.

Most things can be negotiated and employees coming and going from one employment to another should not be afraid to negotiate a better position for themselves.

With a defined benefit pension scheme, at the retirement date of the employee, a pension will be payable based on a formula of years ('N') served with the employer over a pre-determined factor (usually 60ths) times final salary ('FS' – sometimes based on a formula for the final salary or average salary, usually the best three years in the last five or seven years).

The pension was previously limited to 2/3 of the earnings cap (£70,400), which was £105,600 in 2005/06. (However, from 2006/07 the pensions cap has been abolished, and all pension schemes are limited by the SLA – Standard Lifetime Allowance, which in 2010/11 is £1.8 million.)

The above is the formula to be used with at least 20 years service. With less than 20 years service, the maximum pension is scaled down by 1/30th for each year less.

If you joined an employer's scheme before 17th March 1987, then a different maximum accrual rate can apply. This means you could get a maximum 2/3 pension after only ten years (instead of 20 years) service.

Example

Jenny has worked for Excellent Fashions PLC for 25 years before retiring at age 60. She joined the pension scheme on the 1st June 1970. Her pension scheme is a final salary defined benefits scheme. The factor is 60ths. The final salary is based on an average of the best three years out of the last seven years, which in her case are the last three years, averaging £32,000 as a final salary.

Her pension will be: 25 years/60ths x £32,000 per annum.

25/60 x £32,000 = £13,333 gross pension per year. This is within the pensions cap of 2/3 x £105,600 = £70,400, if she had retired before A Day and within the lifetime allowance of £1.8 million fund value if she had retired after A Day (6th April 2006). The pension received is taxable at source at basic rate and Jenny will receive a net pension after tax.

Jenny is also entitled to a tax-free lump sum. The lump sum paid is actually paid from giving up some pension benefits. This is called a commutation.

The maximum tax-free lump sum payable to Jenny depends on when she became a member of the pension scheme, the rules of the particular scheme and her length of service to retirement.

The formula for a tax-free lump sum is based on the greater of 3/80ths of final remuneration for each year of service (up to a maximum of 40 years) or

2.25 times the amount of the member's pension before commutation, whichever is the greater.

This is in turn limited to a maximum tax-free lump sum of 1.5 times final remuneration or 1.5 times the pensions earnings cap, which in 2005/06 was £105,600. This figure x 1.5 = £158,400. If Jenny had waited until after A Day, then she may have applied for primary or enhanced protection of her pension fund, should the tax-free cash amount have been greater under the pre-A Day calculation.

Example (continued)

The formula for Jenny's tax-free lump sum depends on when she joined her employer's pension fund. If she had joined before 1st June 1989 but on or after 17th March 1987, then the maximum tax-free lump sum would be the lesser of £150,000 or 1.5 times remuneration, so long as she had clocked up at least 20 years of service and with a pension of 2/3 of final remuneration.

If she joined the pension scheme before 17th March 1987, then the maximum tax-free lump sum is 1.5 times her final remuneration without any upper limit. However, she must have at least 20 years service at retirement to do so. Lesser service would have a different accrual rate, as it would if Jenny retired early.

In Jenny's case, as she joined the scheme on the 1st June 1970, she would be entitled to the greater of 3/80ths of final remuneration for each year of service or 2.25 times the amount of her pension before commutation, whichever is the greater, so:

3/80 x 25 years x £32,000   = £30,000

or

2.25 x £13,333   = £29,999

Maximum test:
lesser of 1.5 x £32,000   = £48,000

or

1.5 x £105,600   = £158,400 (1.5 times the earnings cap)

The result is that Jenny can take £30,000 tax-free cash, which is well within the maximum tax-free cash allowable to her under the rules as at 5.4.2006. In addition, she would have a pension of £13,333 per annum gross, which is taxable.

2. Defined contribution occupational pension schemes *(money purchase)*

Under these types of pension scheme, the employer determines how much to spend on pension contributions. It is then able to budget for pensions scheme contributions and not incur pension funding liabilities by not being able to adequately fund a pension scheme. Previously these were called 'money purchase pension schemes'.

The type of funding could be as a percentage of employees' pay or even a set fixed figure per employee. Employees can also contribute. You may have a situation, where a scheme is contributory, and the employer pays, say, 10% of salary and the employee 5%; or non-contributory, where the employer pays 10% and the employee nothing. The percentages differ, depending on what can be afforded and agreed between the parties.

The money contributed is invested either through a life office, or fund manager or stockbroker to provide a fund for each employee at the retirement date. Each employee will therefore have a retirement 'pot' containing the company contributions share and his or her own contribution share with any growth in the underlying funds being added.

The pension pot provided for each employee may, at retirement date, be taken as a pension or as a reduced pension and a tax-free lump sum. Alternatively, the tax-free lump sum may be taken and the balance of the fund placed in an income draw-down fund before an alternatively secured pension or annuity is taken by age 75 (77 from 2011/12).

HMRC and pension legislation applies with regard to funding limits, final salary definitions and length of service requirements.

These HMRC limits apply irrespective of whether the scheme is a defined benefits or a defined contribution scheme. With a final salary based defined benefits scheme, the risk of providing a pension and tax-free cash according to the formula, lies with the employer; with a defined contribution scheme, the risk of investment performance and adequate contributions having been made, lies with the employee. The size of the ultimate pension depends on the size of the pension fund, investment performance and quantum of contributions.

Employers can claim their contributions as a corporation tax expense; employees can claim up to 100% of their taxable remuneration (including the value of taxable benefits, such as the company car value) or £255,000, whichever is the less.

Exempt occupational pension schemes do not pay income, corporation or capital gains tax on fund investments. Pension funds cannot reclaim tax credits on dividends from UK companies, which will reduce overall investment returns in any pension fund. This may require schemes to make additional funding to meet pension fund value targets.

At retirement, a taxable pension is paid from the pension fund, usually funded through the internal purchase of an annuity. In addition, a tax-free lump sum is payable, usually at up to 1.5 times final salary, and various rules apply as to maximum amounts (see the section on tax-free lump sums).

Up to A Day (5th April 2006), under the old pension rules, the maximum pension at normal retirement date is limited to £70,400 (2/3 of the pensions earning cap) after 20 years service and the maximum tax-free cash is £158,400. This is because the pensions cap acted as a brake on benefits. After A Day, the pensions cap has been abolished, and a new computation is made. In the 2010/11 tax year, the maximum pension at normal retirement date is limited to £90,000 (1/20th of £1.8 million) using a pension commutation factor of 20 x the pension after 20 years service, and the maximum tax free cash is £450,000 (25% of the fund maximum of £1.8 million). If a member dies before his or her spouse and this is after retirement, then a spouse's pension of up to 2/3 of the member's pension may be payable.

The example given for the defined benefits scheme above, uses the same occupational pension scheme rules for pensions and tax-free lump sums, as well as HMRC limits.

The defined contribution regime

The defined contribution regime includes defined contribution occupational schemes, stakeholder pension schemes and personal pension schemes.

From 6th April 2001 to 5th April 2006, members of a defined benefit scheme (final salary) could contribute to a defined contribution regime scheme (money purchase, such as stakeholder or personal pension scheme) where:

(i) earnings for any of the previous five tax years have not exceeded £30,000 (but not taking into account tax years before 2000/01)

(ii) the individual concerned has not been a controlling director during the current or five preceding tax years

What this means is that you can contribute a maximum additional amount because of the stakeholder pension rules of £3,600, in addition to the 15% of earnings to a defined benefit scheme as an employee. The maximum limit to contribute under the earnings cap for the 15% was £15,840 in 2005/06. These additional benefits are ignored when calculating the overall maximum benefits from the defined benefit scheme (i.e. the main pension scheme), but AVC benefits are included in the calculation. After A Day, 6th April 2006, you, the employee can contribute to any number of pension schemes (your main employer scheme, a stakeholder scheme, AVC and personal pension scheme), as long as it is within the £255,000 annual allowance and up to 100% of salary. The previous rules as to £30,000 earnings and controlling director status fall away under the new regime.

3. AVC/FSAVC

Additional Voluntary Contributions (AVC) are paid in addition to normal employer scheme contributions, to secure extra benefits. The AVC is offered by the same pension provider to the main pension scheme and is administered by the employer. The free-standing AVC, (FSAVC), can be purchased from any product provider and gives more investment control to the individual.

Under the new rules from 6th April 2006, all AVC schemes may allow 25% of the fund value to be taken as tax-free cash. Benefits can also be taken as income drawdown, and you need not buy an annuity. The AVC scheme was very inflexible under the old regime as the AVC scheme combined with your occupational pension could give rise to excessive benefits, with tax charged on any excess refunds at 32%. Under the new regime, total benefits from all schemes are only limited by the lifetime limit.

Contributions are tax deductible up to 100% of your remuneration, capped at £255,000 in 2010/11. Contributions are paid net of basic rate tax, thus saving cash flow. If a higher rate taxpayer, the balance of relief at 20% is claimed through your tax return.

With the advent of the stakeholder pension regime and the grouping together of various defined contribution pension plans under one umbrella, employees may make contributions into AVCs, and FSAVCs at 100% of remuneration as defined up to £255,000 in 2010/11, which may include £3,600 gross (£2,880) net in a stakeholder pension scheme. As most employees do not have sufficient cash available to invest into both stakeholder pension plans and an FSAVC, and because stakeholder offered far more flexible options, including tax-free cash, the trend has been for employees to contribute to a stakeholder plan rather than to FSAVCs. However, if they can afford it, they can contribute to both, and stakeholder benefits will be aggregated with occupational scheme benefits when the maximum lifetime allowance tests are being completed.

An FSAVC may be used for individual contracting out purposes from the S2P (the State Second Pension). This may be the case even where the employer's scheme is contracted in. A percentage between 1.6% and 3.7% could be paid to the employee's FSAVC as a contracting out rebate. However, as HMRC gives tax relief on the employee's share of the rebate if paid to a personal pension plan (but not to a FSAVC), most would go the PPP route for the grossed up rebate to maximise their personal positions.

4. Small self-administered pension schemes (SSAS)

A SSAS is an approved occupational pension scheme with defined contributions. It must have fewer than 12 members (i.e. a maximum of 11 members). Prior to A Day, a SSAS was only available to company members – after A Day, it is available to partners and LLP members.

Traditionally the costs of running a SSAS have been higher than a group of SIPPs, for example, with costs at up to £1,250 a year or more, depending on the scheme and its investments, accounting policies and trustees. It is usually set up by controlling directors of family companies who wish to have personal control over scheme investments, including shares in the company.

After A Day, SSAS pension funds are part of the unified regime and their investments are the same as SIPPs (covered previously under the SIPP section). Different investment rules applied previously to SIPPs and SSAS investments. The new rules may not allow certain transactions in the same way that the previous rules did. One example is with respect to borrowings by the SSAS to purchase a property or make loans – usually to the employer company, or to purchase shares.

Borrowings

Trustees can borrow money so long as it used to benefit the pension scheme.

A SSAS could borrow a maximum amount pre-A Day of 45% of the current value of the scheme plus 3 x the average of the last three years' contributions. Post A Day, the maximum amount that can be borrowed is 50% of the current value of the scheme, less any outstanding loans.

As mentioned in the previous chapter, changes to the tax rules announced 15th April 2009 allow SIPPs and SSASs to restructure their borrowing terms on loans made against more than 50% of the fund's value without a tax penalty, so long as the amount borrowed is not increased. Leases on commercial property held by the pension scheme can also be re-negotiated allowing reduced rental to be paid, even where the property is let to connected members. Tax charges are also waived on loans where residential property is used as collateral.

Property purchase

The SSAS can invest in commercial property (not residential property), and can now purchase the property from a connected party. The SSAS can use its own funds, or make borrowings to do so.

Post A Day the maximum amount that can be borrowed is 50% of the current value of the scheme, less any outstanding loans.

If a property is to be purchased then 100% of scheme assets plus any scheme borrowings can be used, making it 150% of the scheme's current value. Apart from property, borrowed money can be used for stocks and shares.

If for example, a pension fund is currently valued at £700,000, then 50% of the value of the scheme is £350,000 that can be borrowed.

Buying the business premises could make sense. The rental income accruing is tax-free in the hands of the pension fund, and when the property is sold there is no capital gains tax payable, therefore all growth in the property is tax-free. The rental payments are deductible to the business for tax purposes. Compare this to an individual owning a commercial property. Rental income is taxable, and the property is subject to capital gains on sale and inheritance tax on death.

Lending money

A SSAS can lend money to any unconnected third party – individual or company. It can make a loan to a sponsoring employer, but not to connected parties. Up to 50% of the total net assets of the SSAS can be loaned after two years – 25% below two years of the existence of the SSAS. The loan must be for no longer than 5 years. The interest rate must be a minimum of 1% to 3% above base rate, and loaned monies must be repaid by equal instalments of interest and capital. The trustees make the loan, not the member. Stringent conditions apply.

Businesses borrowing funds from a SSAS could be doubling up on tax reliefs. The Government has boosted the annual investment allowance to £100,000 (from £50,000). The business borrows £100,000 from the SSAS and invests in plant and machinery. The business gets tax relief on repaying the loan to the pension scheme, as well as tax relief on investing in plant and machinery.

Investments

See the section on SIPPs which have equal investment possibilities applying to SSASs.

In general, the new pensions regime will drive life into the SSAS and SIPP pensions market place. The lifting of the pensions cap and onerous restrictions on funding and high charges will introduce greater funds than before into SSAS and SIPP schemes. As a form of corporate tax planning, a business investing deductible profits into pension schemes could reduce their own corporate tax rates, whilst using pensions for profit extraction.

A SSAS can invest up to 5% of the fund value in the shares in the sponsoring company. A SSAS could potentially own 100% of the company's shares so long as the value does not exceed 5% of the value of the SSAS.

7

Stakeholder Pensions

Description

The Stakeholder pension scheme was introduced through the Welfare Reform and Pensions Act 1999. It is the plain vanilla version of a personal pension plan, and designed to enable a pension to be possible for all. In fact, for the first time, the concept of having to have 'net relevant earnings' to contribute to a pension scheme is swept away, and non-earning spouses and children can now have a pension scheme.

Premium contributions

The stakeholder pension scheme is designed to give pension benefits to those retiring between ages 55 and 75 (77 from 2011/12). Premiums can be regular (with a minimum of £20) or single premiums and in both cases cannot exceed £3,600 gross per annum without reference to earnings. There is no frequency of premium payment, so long as the minimum of £20 is made each time.

Where there is reference to earnings, then contributions in excess of the £3,600 will be allowed in accordance with current annual allowances for contributions, which is 100% of earnings up to £255,000.

If a member of an occupational pension scheme

If you are an employee with an occupational pension scheme, then you may contribute to both that scheme and to a personal pension or stakeholder pension scheme. Your annual allowance is 100% of salary up to £255,000 in 2010/11 tax year.

For example, an employee earning say £25,000 can be a member of an occupational pension scheme, contribute £3,600 (net £2,880) to a stakeholder pension scheme, and the balance of contributions as a percentage of taxable earnings to an AVC or FSAVC scheme.

It should be borne in mind that stakeholder costs will be lower than most other schemes. To this extent, most will prefer the stakeholder pension route, rather than the FSAVC/AVC route for both the £3,600 and the balance % of taxable earnings. Stakeholder is generally being used in preference to the FSAVC pension as being more flexible and cheaper.

At retirement, the total value of all pension funds from all schemes is taken into account when calculating the overall maximum benefits.

Who can take out a stakeholder pension?

You can take out the pension scheme yourself, or take one out for someone else, such as a child or grandchild. Alternatively, an employer can set up or designate a scheme (in fact, legally all employers with 4 or more employees must designate a stakeholder pension scheme or face large fines).

It is most suitable for self-employed individuals, or those employees who are not in an occupational pension scheme. If you are an employee in an occupational pension scheme, you can also have a stakeholder scheme (in addition to your occupational scheme membership).

Pensions flexibility means you can provide dependants with a pension scheme. Even a baby can have a pension scheme, and need never make a pension contribution ever again – you as parent or grandparent can build up a tax efficient fund for a child.

For example, minors can invest £3,600 a year each into a stakeholder pension without the need for earnings. As pension contributions are made net of basic rate tax of 20%, you need only invest £2,880 to have an actual investment of £3,600.

If you invest £234 net per month into a stakeholder or SIPP for a child from birth to age 60, with a growth rate of 7% per annum and a 1% charge, the pension fund value would be £1.54 million – if you ceased payments by the time the child was age 18, the fund would be worth £1.26 million by age 60. The premiums should decrease your estate for inheritance tax purposes (you can gift £3,000 pa and make unlimited payments from normal expenditure not required by you).

Tax relief on contributions

All contributions are paid into your stakeholder pension plan net of basic rate tax. This applies to those with no income, as well as the self-employed. The contribution increases your basic tax rate band.

If you wish to contribute £100 per month, then you only actually pay £80 and HMRC pays £20. Basic rate of tax is 20% in 2010/11.

A higher-rate tax payer can deduct a further 20% of his gross contribution through his tax return.

Contracting out of State Second Pension – S2P

Age related rebates to stakeholder schemes are possible for those contracting out and for any stakeholder scheme, the rebate is based on the stakeholder's actual salary in excess of the lower earnings limit (even though the State Second Pension will be based on £9,500. You can only contract out if employed and earning a salary).

Life cover

Pension term to age 75 provided for tax-deductible premiums before December 2006. Tax-deductible premiums only apply to existing policies, not new ones after that date. Contributions are made net of basic rate tax and if a higher rate taxpayer, an additional 20% is claimed through your tax return. There is no limit to the amount of pension term life cover you could have had, other than actuarial limitations and not to have a fund greater than the SLA – the standard lifetime allowance, which was £1.5 million in 2006/07 and is now £1.8 million in 2010/11.

A Stakeholder pension cannot have a waiver of premium benefit incorporated into it. Waiver of premium can be a stand-alone policy though and is always advisable if you can get it. What it does is protect you if you become disabled and cannot work nor pay premiums as a result. The pension contributions are paid for you. This separate contract is not tax deductible, but the premiums are usually very small, and tax relief would have been negligible.

The pension fund itself

The contributions are made to the pension fund. They are paid net of basic rate tax, even for non-earners. Once in the pension fund, these contributions are invested into the selected investment accounts where the growth is tax-free. HMRC pays in the balance being the basic rate tax amount of 20%.

The widely publicised minimum standards for stakeholder pensions means that the maximum charge will be 1% of the fund value per annum. No other charges from the fund will be allowed.

There may well be other charges – for advice or other services – but these have to be paid for separately, not from the fund.

Most types of investment options are available, including with profits.

At retirement

Retirement can be between the ages of 55 and 75 (77 from 2011/12). At retirement, you have a choice of either taking 25% in cash tax-free from the fund with a reduced annuity (or pension), or taking a full pension, with no tax-free cash. Alternatively, you can go into drawdown and draw income from your fund until age 75 when you must take an annuity or an ASP (Alternatively Secured Pension). The pension or annuity taken is taxable. Much will depend on your circumstances at retirement, as to which option is to be taken up.

The retirement date can be flexible and you do not need to actually retire to receive your benefits.

Death before retirement

If you die before retirement, then death benefits could be a return of fund plus interest, and any amount insured for under the contract.

Employer's responsibilities

Employers with 5 or less employees are exempt from providing stakeholder access. They are also exempt if there is an occupational pension scheme, so long as employees can join within 12 months of starting work. Those under age 18 or within 5 years of retirement can also be excluded.

Another employer exemption is where the employer has a Group Personal Pension Scheme (GPP), contributes at least 3% of basic pay, has no exit penalties, and is available within 3 months of joining the employer (except if under age 18).

Other exemptions also apply. For example, where employees earn below the lower earnings limit, stakeholder does not have to be offered to them. One would think this is the very group that stakeholder pensions should be directed at, but the Government obviously feels they cannot afford even the most basic pension contribution.

If the employer is not exempt, then it must offer access to a stakeholder scheme within 3 months of joining the employer.

The employer need only designate a scheme (choose a prospective supplier), not operate a scheme, or recommend one. The employer then consults with employees as to the proposed designated scheme, giving them necessary information; operates a payroll system to deduct contributions from pay; and maintains stakeholder compliance.

The new compulsory pension regime from 2012 for all employees (NEST) will make much of the stakeholder provision redundant. Employers will need to enrol all employees automatically into a NEST scheme, unless already offering a suitable scheme. Employees will contribute 4% of band earnings (between £5,000 and £33,000) and employers 3%, with 1 I% coming from tax relief. A total of 8% of band earnings will need to be paid into a NEST pension scheme or alternative by 2012. Enrolment will be staggered from 2012 to 2016.

The National Employment Savings Trust (NEST) – will allow tax relief for employee and employer contributions from the date of the next Finance Act.

Stakeholder investment strategies

If aged over 55, then contribute £2,880. HMRC increases this to £3,600. Take 25% of £3,600 in tax-free cash (£900). This gives an immediate guaranteed return of 25% plus your tax relief – total returns could be 45% (basic rate taxpayer) or 60% (higher rate), plus a deferred pension. Anyone can do it each year for the best guaranteed rates in the market place.

8

State Pension Scheme

There is no actuarially funded state pension scheme, like an employer's pension scheme. Those in work pay in national insurance contributions at a predetermined amount, those on state pensions receive their share as the state pension weekly or monthly.

The state provides pension funds in two distinct parts. The first part is the 'old age pension' or the basic state scheme; the second part is known State Second Pension (S2P) – previously SERPS (until April 2002).

The *Pensions Act* 2007 reformed the state pension system. It will make the state pension more generous, fairer to women and carers and more widely available.

Key changes are as follows:

- From 2010 the number of years to qualify for a state pension will reduce from 39 years for women and 44 years for men to 30 years for both. Currently around 65% of women fail to qualify for a full basic state pension. These changes should enable up to 75% of women to qualify.
- From 2012 the basic state pension will be linked to annual cost of living increases in earnings rather than prices (RPI). [*This has gone further, with a triple lock in from 2010 of earnings, prices and 2.5% minimum*].
- The contribution conditions will be changed to make it easier to build up an entitlement to a basic state pension.
- Home Responsibilities Protection (HRP) will be replaced with a new system of weekly credits for those caring for children up to the age of 12 and for those who spend at least 20 hours a week caring for severely disabled people.

The state pension age is currently 65 for men and 60 for women. It will be equalised upwards for women to age 65 from April 2010. Women will have to work an extra 5 years before the state pension benefits them in the future. The gradual increase in female state pension age to 65 begins from the start of the 2010/11 tax year. It should be fully equalised by April 2020 with the men's SPA (state pension age).

The new pension age of 65 for all will affect women born after April 1955. Women born after April 1950 and before April 1955 will have a state pension age of between 60 and 65. Women born before April 1950 will have a state pension age of 60. The Government is considering removing the default retirement age of 65, but this will not be before 2011. The state pension age is expected to increase up to age 68 in gradual stages.

The Government has begun a process to make people more aware that they must provide for their own retirement and supplement the state pensions, as these will not be adequate for their needs.

The average amount a couple received from an occupational pension scheme in 2005/2006 was £192 p.m., and it's not much different now in 2010. Life expectancy has increased to 16.6 years for men at the age of 65, and 19.6 years for women at the age of 65.

In addition, the state pension age will be gradually increased to reach age 68 for both men and women by 2046 [now by 2024], as it is generally believed that people are living longer. Of interest is that there are now more people age over 65 in the UK than those aged under 16. The demographics of this is that not only are people working well into retirement, but that there will be fewer people working to support those in retirement. To meet this heavier state pension burden it is inevitable that national insurance contributions will rise rapidly in the future, and the state will seek to shift the future pensions' burden onto employers through compulsion from 2012 with NEST.

What is it worth?

In 2010/11 the basic State Pension is as follows:

Claimant   £97.65 per week (£5077.80 p.a.)
Adult dependant £58.50 per week (£3042 p.a.)
Total married   £156.15 per week (£8,119.80 p.a.)
Or civil partnership where the wife/civil partner was a non-contributor.

The basic state pension increases by 2.5% from April 2010. The Government confirmed a triple guarantee for the basic state pension. From April 2010 it will be increased by the higher of the increase in prices, earnings or 2.5%.

There are other state pensions, for example for widows. To qualify for a maximum state pension you need to have paid national insurance for about 90% of your working lifetime – or have been exempt during child-rearing years (with home responsibilities protection), for example. One of the proposals for reform was to reduce the qualifying period to 30 years from around 40 years, [which happened from 6.4.2010]. This was in the Pensions Act 2007.

The state basic pension has been rising each year by the RPI as at September in each year and applied from April of the following year. Up to April 2010, increases in the state basic pension after retirement are linked to the RPI – the retail prices index – and not the AEI, the average earnings index, which rises at a higher rate. Benefits were therefore worth less than if they were linked to the AEI. A pensions reform proposal was to reintroduce the link between state pension increases and average earnings in 2012 (or sooner). This has now happened with the Budget announcement in June 2010, two years earlier than expected. From time to time, the Government increases retirement pay with winter fuel allowances and other vote catching payments.

Can you take early or late retirement?

You can, but don't expect anything from the state until the designated day arrives at 65 for men and 60 for women currently.

However, you can postpone your state retirement benefits from retirement age onwards for a slightly higher benefit for each year deferred. From April 2005, extra state pension may be earned at 1% for every 5 weeks deferral, which equates to 10.4% for each year; alternatively for a minimum pension deferral of 12 months, a taxable lump sum may be paid, based on the pension foregone, with interest compounded. You can now defer for as long as you like, and you can even defer a state pension, once you have started taking it, providing you do so within the first 5 years after retirement. Lump sums payable in this way will be taxable at your marginal rates of tax, but will not affect entitlement to age relief.

Can you take a lump sum?

Apart from your deferral lump sum above, no lump sum rights can be accrued. There is no tax-free lump sum, nor can the state scheme be commuted for a lump sum, nor is there a death in service lump sum. However, there are very small bereavement allowances, should you die in the tax year. Every little bit helps, but don't get too excited as the amounts are small.

The maximum pension is achieved by making contributions during 90% of your working life between ages 16 to 65. If you are not at that level, then voluntary contributions can be made to get there. However, these voluntary contributions are not tax deductible to you.

Buying back years in the state pension scheme is possible, to boost income in retirement. Establish your shortfall through completing Form BR 19 available from the Pensions' Service at www.pensionservice.gov.uk or write to the address below.

Who to contact

Apply to the Department for Work & Pensions, for form BR19 to establish what your pension benefits are. You can call them on 0845 3000 168 or write to:

Retirement Pension Forecasting Team
The Pension Service
Whitley Road
Newcastle upon Tyne
NE98 1BA

9

SERPS and S2P
and the Pension Credit

The State Earnings Related Pension Scheme (SERPS) was the additional component to the basic state pension scheme, and was replaced by S2P, the State Second Pension Scheme in April 2002. Under the White Paper reforms, S2P will be simplified as a *'flat rate weekly top-up to the basic state pension' which will pay at least £135 a week by 2050.'* (John Hutton, Secretary of state for Work and Pensions, 25.5.2006 in a statement to the Commons).

SERPS was not and the S2P is not available to the self-employed, only to those in employment.

To reduce reliance on the state Schemes, the Government allows employees to contract out of S2P. Contracting out rebates do not count towards the annual pension allowance for contributions. National insurance rebates from both employer and employee can be paid to an individual's own personal pension plan or FSAVC, either on their own, or along with other contributions made by the individual, or to the employer's scheme. If rebates are due to your own personal pension scheme, these are paid by HMRC – you and the employer continue to pay full national insurance contributions. Rebates of national insurance contributions for salary related schemes in 2010/11 are 3.7% for employers and 1.6% for employees. If you are a member of a money purchase scheme (defined contributions), then the employer must make minimum payments into the scheme equal to the combined employee/employer rebates of 2.6%. This is 1% for the employer and 1.6% for the employee. HMRC tops up the payments by age-related rebates up to a maximum combined figure of 10.5% at age 55 or over in the 2006/07 tax year (less for ages 59-60). From the 2007/08 tax year, the maximum combined rebate was reduced to 7.4%. The process is complicated and different rebate amounts depend on what sort of scheme you are in and your age.

Contracted out employees receive the basic state pension, but instead of S2P or SERPS, receive an additional pension from their employer's scheme, or their personal pension schemes.

It will be possible to contract out of S2P in the following way:

* Enhanced rebate benefit under personal pension schemes

- For a stakeholder pension the rebate is based on the stakeholder's actual salary in excess of the lower earnings limit, although the State Second Pension will be based on £9,500.
- For occupational money purchase schemes (COMPS) and contracted out salary related schemes (COSRS), the position is more or less the same as under SERPS, but the level of rebates is growing smaller over time and the Government wishes to phase rebating out under its pension reforms.

Contracting back in

If there has been poor investment performance in individual pension plans, you may be advised to contract back in to S2P. Alternatively, you could consider transferring your contracted-out pension funds to a lower-costed pension contract. Some of the old contracts could have funds of around £40,000 in them, and lower costs and improved investment performance could improve your position.

Some pension providers, have told their contracted-out personal pension policyholders to contract back in to S2P or find an alternative provider. Anyone aged over 43 will lose out financially through being contracted out under post-April 2007 rebate rates. The break-even age to receive more than from contracting in will fall to 43.

However, the facts are that SERPS has been reduced 3 times for men and 4 for women; the Government has stated its intention to change S2P to a flat rate scheme - this might affect S2P entitlements prior to such a change; pensions reform could mean scrapping S2P and increasing the basic state pension with accrued S2P entitlements being lost. The decision to contract out or not, or to contract back in is based on whether investment performance can beat what you may get under S2P. You will need a calculation based on your attitude to investment risk, flexibility of benefits (if you died, your heirs could get a return of fund, whereas under S2P the benefit is lost); your marital status at retirement, and whether you believe the Government will keep its promises.

However, the *Pensions Act 2007* included measures to abolish contracting out for defined contribution money purchase occupational pension schemes and personal and stakeholder pension schemes.

The *Pensions Act 2007* introduced national insurance credits from 2010 for those with long-term disabilities and people with caring responsibilities so that they can build up additional pension entitlements.

State second pension (S2P)

The S2P accrual is based on a percentage of band earnings. Currently this is based on three salary tiers and is calculated on 10%, 20% and 40% of each tier's earnings. Proposals in the *Pensions Act 2007* reforms S2P to become a simple flat rate weekly top up to the basic State Pension by 2030.

The upper accruals point for S2P is introduced from April 2009 (as opposed to 2010). The upper earnings limit is replaced by the Upper Accrual Point for S2P and is fixed at £770 per week (£40,040 p.a.) This has been frozen and renamed upper accrual point to facilitate the gradual withdrawal of the 10% accrual band.

Band earnings for S2P in 2010/11 are as follows:
Lower earnings limit: £97 per week (£5,044 p.a.)
Upper earnings limit: £770 per week (£40,040).

The accrual rate for middle and upper bands of S2P will merge into one band accruing at 10% in respect of band earnings between £14,100 and £40,040.
Salary sacrifice for individuals with income above the upper earnings accrual point of £40,040 may be attractive as there is no loss of S2P benefit for earnings sacrificed above that level. (Employees pay NI at the full rate up to the upper earnings limit of £43,875, but S2P only accrues to the Upper Accrual Point (UAP) of £40,040. Between these two points employees pay full Ni with no additional S2P benefit – a good reason for salary sacrifice down to the UAP in return for an employer pension contribution of the same amount.]
If an employee has earnings above the NI lower earnings level (LEL) of £5,044 p.a. but below the lower earnings threshold (LET) – currently £14,100 – any S2P benefit will be based on a notional salary equalling the LET in all cases. Where earnings are between these two levels, it may be beneficial to use salary sacrifice to take salaries down to the LEL. This will have no effect on their S2P rights, but they will make savings from NI contributions from their salary. These savings with employer's NI savings can increase pension contributions.

The pension credit

Pensions Credit
Guarantee Credit
Single	£132.60	(£6,895.20 pa)
Couple	£202.40	(£10,524.80)

Savings Credit threshold
Single	£98.40
Couple	£157.25

The age of entitlement for a guarantee credit payment will gradually increase from age 60 to 65 by 2020.
The pension credit was introduced in October 2003. The pension credit is an entitlement for people aged 60 or over living in the UK. Pension Credit guarantees everyone age 60 and over an income of at least £132.60 per

week if single and £202.40 per week if you have a partner (including civil partnerships).

Earnings against which the provision of S2P is measured have been capped at an upper accrual point fixed at £770 p.w. (£40,040 p.a.) from the 2009/10 tax year. As a result there will be increased NI contributions payable.

The minimum guaranteed entitlement will be linked to growth in average earnings. What this means is that if your qualifying income is less than the pensions credit then a payment can be made to you.

The standard minimum guarantee rises to £132.60 for single pensioners and £202.40 for couples in 2010/11. Every person aged over 60 will be guaranteed at least £6,895.20 per annum if single and £10,524.80 if married.

There are two elements – the guarantee credit element (which guarantees a minimum income if you are on a low income and age 60) and the savings credit element (if age 65 +, as a reward for saving for your retirement). The savings element intends to reward those who have saved towards retirement, by increasing the individual's income by an additional 60p for every £1 of income in excess of the basic state pension (where that income comes from private pension schemes, part-time earnings and so on). The maximum possible savings credit is £20.52 per week for a single person and £27.09 for a couple in the 2010/11 tax year. There could be more money available to you (an additional £52.85 per week) if you are severely disabled, look after someone who is severely disabled and have certain housing costs. From November 2009, the capital disregard for pension credit and pensioner related Housing and Council Tax benefit increased from £6,000 to £10,000.

To apply for pension credit call 0800 99 1234. Further updated information is available from www.thepensionservice.gov.uk/pensioncredit and www.direct.gov.uk

10

Tax-Free Cash Lump Sums

Most pension funds provide the opportunity to commute part of the pension funds for tax-free cash. There are different rules for different funds up to A-Day on how tax-free cash is calculated and treated. Most financial advisers will tell clients to always take the tax-free cash. The reason is that it immediately provides for a diversification of assets. In addition, if an annuity is required, then a voluntarily purchased one using tax-free cash would be more tax efficient than a pension annuity. However, with annuity rates low, mostly alternative income-producing investments will be used.

Cash may be required to pay off debts, make gifts to family members, pay for that holiday of a lifetime, keeping the business going, university and school fees, refurbishing the house, settling divorce commitments and making investments.

Benefits accrued up to A Day, including tax-free cash lump sums can be ring-fenced under primary or enhanced protection, especially if tax-free cash may be more than 25% of the fund value. After A Day, tax-free cash (now called the pension commencement lump sum or PCLS) may not exceed 25% of the value of the fund up to the lifetime allowance at retirement date (currently £1.8 million in 2010/11 and 25% will be £450,000 as a maximum tax-free cash lump sum. Tax-free cash must be taken before age 75 (if you fail to take it by then, you will be stopped from doing so).

Different pension schemes at different times have formulae for calculating tax-free cash, and this will continue to be the case. However, unless protected, after A Day, you cannot have more than 25% of the fund value as tax-free cash.

The following pension schemes provide tax-free lump sums.

Final salary scheme pension fund/occupational pension schemes

1. The position *after 1st June 1989* is as follows:

- Maximum tax-free cash is the greater of 3/80ths of final remuneration for each year of service (maximum of 40 years), or 2.25 times the amount of the member's pension before commutation.

- This is limited to the lesser of 1.5 times final remuneration, or 1.5 times the earnings cap (£158,400 for 2005/06).(note the earnings cap falls away after A Day).

2. Final salary pension schemes members *between 17th March 1987 and 1st June 1989* are limited to a maximum tax-free lump sum of £150,000 or 1.5 times remuneration, whichever is the less (with 20+ years service and where the pension is 2/3 of final remuneration). One can only get maximum lump sum benefits if maximum pension benefits are taken.

3. Final salary schemes members *before 17.3.1987* have 1.5 times remuneration without any upper limit. However, they must have 20 years service to get this.

For all of the above there may be different accrual rates dependant on service and other factors (like the pension scheme rules) and advice may be required.

Defined contribution pension schemes, personal pension plans, stakeholder pension plans, group personal pension plans

These have 25% of the accumulated pension fund that may be taken as a cash lump sum, free of tax (but now including protected rights portion of the fund).

Protected rights funds

Only up to 25% of the fund could be taken as tax-free cash, even if the scheme member is entitled to a higher amount. If the protected rights form part of a pensions credit transfer for divorce purposes, (called safeguarded rights) you cannot take tax-free cash from them.

FSAVCs and AVCs

You can now have 25% of the FSAVC/AVC fund in tax- free cash (after A Day).

Retirement annuities (Sec 226)

3 times the residual annuity may be taken as tax-free cash. This may be higher than the 25% for personal pension plans above and should be ring-fenced under primary or enhanced protection. However, if the open-market option is used by the annuitant to increase the annuity payable, then the tax-

free cash amount reduces to 25%, as the retirement annuity must be transferred to a personal pension plan first before the cash can be taken. It may be tax efficient, if over age 55 from 6th April 2010, to invest into a personal pension plan, obtain tax relief on the contributions and to immediately take the tax-free cash. This cash could again be used for gearing purposes, for example to invest into a tax-reducing VCT (venture capital trust), or even to reduce credit card debt.

Recycling of tax-free cash

To prevent pension funds from being boosted by the recycling of tax-free cash lump sums and the claiming of tax reliefs, anti-avoidance rules were brought in at A Day. This applies to lump sums paid on or after 6th April 2006. The provisions do not apply where:

- no more than 30% of the lump sum is recycled
- if total lump sums received within 12 months do not exceed 1% of the lifetime allowance (£18,000 in 2010/11)

If you do recycle, then the penalties are that the lump sum recycled is treated as an unauthorised pension payment, liable to tax at up to 55%, plus a scheme sanction charge – up to 95% altogether. If you pre-planned to make the contribution before taking the tax-free cash, this is also caught by the recycling rules, as well as taking loans to fund contributions or increased employer contributions.

However, there is nothing to stop you from taking your tax-free cash and investing it elsewhere, such as a VCT or EIS investment to obtain tax reliefs. So you can recycle your money, but not into pension funds.

Taking the tax-free cash

You can take part or all of your tax-free cash lump sum after age 55 and leave the balance of your fund to grow tax-free. You can spend the money without having to stop work and retiring in the full sense of the word.

However, you could lose the benefit of tax-free future growth on the money. This argument is offset if you are clearing expensive debt though. Research has shown that 35% of retirees will go travelling on their tax-free cash, 33% will pay off a mortgage, and 21% will help their children onto the property ladder.

Taking tax-free cash may be easy from a personal pension plan, but not from a stakeholder plan – if only taking the cash now, you would have to transfer to a PPP first and then take the cash from there, the balance of your fund going into drawdown (you take nil drawdown if you do not want income at that time). Be careful though – your fund may be making an unauthorised payment if an unsecured pension (USP) or 'relevant pension' is not possible from your particular scheme. Check with the product provider first before opting for tax-free cash only with a deferred pension or drawdown later. It appears that you cannot move to another scheme for the USP or annuity once the tax-free cash has been taken – it must remain with the same scheme.

Beware though taking tax-free cash early from some schemes, such as a final salary scheme, because the value of the income you are giving up is greater than the amount of lump sum, in most cases. There could be hidden costs (you may have to move to another pension scheme to take out your cash); or the fund rules may not allow you to do so (even the legislation allows this under A Day); under-funded occupational schemes may give you a bad deal if you take early retirement in this way. Always check the figures first, before acting.

Trivial commutations

If your total pension funds do not come to more than £18,000 in 2010/11, you can commute them for cash. You must be age 60 and over to do this. 25% of the amount commuted will be tax-free, the balance is taxable as income. If a basic rate taxpayer, 75% of your fund will be taxed at 20%, a higher rate taxpayer at 40%. The limit is set at 1% of the lifetime allowance and rises each year. One can now also have trivial commutations of company pension schemes where the value of the benefits is below £2,000, and this is in addition to the 1% allowance.

Changes to pension commencement lump sum (PCLS)
(otherwise known as tax-free cash)

From 6th April 2006 paras 9-11 of Schedule 20 of the *Finance Act 2007* extend the period within which a PCLS may be paid free of tax to any time within an 18 month period starting 6 months before and ending 12 months after the date when the member becomes entitled to the related pension. The entitlement to the PCLS must have arisen before age 75. If you die having taken the lump sum but before taking the pension, entitlement to the lump sum is deemed to have arisen immediately before death. There is also now a 2 year time limit on the payment of lump sum death benefits of the scheme being notified of the member's death.

The *Finance Act 2008* amends the way in which the pension commencement lump sum is calculated where transitional protection is applied to that lump sum. This applies to both defined benefit and defined contribution schemes and increases the lump sum tax free cash payments for some DC and DB members and section 32 members who have protected cash. It also removes the need to check whether a top-up contribution is needed before drawing benefits. Do not then add further contributions where the arrangement has tax free cash. If fund growth is below the increase in lifetime allowance, a separate arrangement will produce more tax free cash from additional contributions.

11

FURBS or EFRBS – Unapproved Retirement Benefit Schemes

Many executives have used a FURBS to provide a tax-free cash benefit as a top up to normal pension funding. Pre-A Day (6th April 2006), a FURBS could be reasonably tax efficient – post-A Day, there are no tax advantages and the resulting lump sum becomes taxable. The portion built up pre-A Day is in accordance with the old rules; whilst post-A Day contributions and the fund produced will be taxable.

Description

A Funded Unapproved Retirement Benefit Scheme, a FURBS, is an employer contribution scheme, usually for those with earnings in excess of the earnings cap which applied up to 2005/06. The earnings cap for 2005/06 was £105,600.

This meant that regular pensions contributions could only be made on earnings up to the earnings cap level. Above that level, the employer may contribute to a FURBS (a funded scheme) or an UURBS (an unfunded retirement benefit scheme.) Now we have an EFRBS – an employer funded retirement benefit scheme.

However, this need not always be the case (only suitable if earnings are above the earnings cap) and cases have been known of FURBS being taken out below the earnings cap. A FURBS today, when there is no pensions cap, other than the lifetime allowance of £1.8 million (and annual allowance of £255,000) enables a high earner to build up alternative investments outside normal pension funding.

Pre-A Day Position (pre 6th April 2006)

There are two types of unapproved schemes available.

The Funded Unapproved Retirement Benefit Scheme (FURBS)

The employer set up a trust and made contributions to the trust, which was for the benefit of the employee. The trust can invest in any type of investment permitted by the scheme, and there are few investment constraints.

The retirement date is flexible and need not be aligned to any other pension scheme's retirement date. Usually, though retirement is by age 75.

The employer's contributions are allowable against profits in the year paid, as expended 'wholly and exclusively for the purposes of trade'.

The employee pays tax on the contribution under employment income (previously Schedule E). The contribution made by the employer is, however, treated as relevant earnings for any exempt approved scheme. This means that FURBS contributions increase your pensionable pay for higher levels of normal pension contributions to other funds.

Employer national insurance is payable on the contributions made.

The main reason why people took out a FURBS was that for a higher rated taxpayer, investment income was taxed at 20%, and UK dividends and interest were taxed at 20%. In addition, in the FURBS, capital gains tax was payable at the trust rate of 18%, and capital gains could be deferred. Significant tax and investment planning could therefore produce a reasonable investment fund.

The use of offshore funds meant that gross roll-up non-distributor investment funds could be used (as tax is only charged when the fund is sold or disposed of) thus further enhancing the investment possibilities.

At retirement, the whole fund could be taken as tax-free cash. Alternatively, an annuity can be taken with the fund proceeds. This would be a voluntary purchase annuity (essentially using your own tax paid capital), with further tax advantages.

FURBS were popular with those wishing to defer their bonus payments into an eventual tax-free cash lump. The FURBS did give a tax-free benefit and designated the employee by name as a beneficiary, unlike an EBT which is wholly discretionary. FURBS therefore had distinct benefits over an EBT (Employee Benefits Trust).

Unfunded Unapproved Retirement Benefit Scheme (UURBS)

This is a tax paid scheme. The employer makes a contribution, usually tax relievable, and the employee is taxed on it as income. Employer NI is payable on the contributions.

Essentially, the scheme is a notional one only. It would arise where, for example, the employee has not built up a pension scheme, the employer pays a lump sum and/or a 'pension' to the employee to give the employee a retirement benefit.

Post-A Day (6th April 2006) position

There were transitional provisions in relation to tax-free lump sum rights at 6th April 2006. Funds accumulated through a FURB to A Day will be on the old basis, after A Day an apportionment will take place in respect of further contributions. Unregistered schemes are termed 'employer-financed retirement benefit schemes' – EFRBS- (under FA 2006). Employers will not receive tax relief for pension contributions until benefits are paid out of the fund; employees will not be taxed on the employer contributions; income in the fund will be taxed at the 50% trust rate (42.5% for dividends). Capital gains are now taxed at 28% without indexation and taper reliefs. When the benefits are taken from the fund by the employee, the employee will be taxed on those benefits at marginal rates of tax.

Essentially therefore, the main benefit would be that the employee is not taxed on the contributions made by the employer as a benefit in kind (whereas prior to A Day, the employee was so taxed and NICs were payable on the contributions). However, whereas previously a tax-free lump sum could arise, now the lump sum is taxable.

Also, any employer contributions and accrued funds will not affect the lifetime allowance nor the annual allowance.

Why invest in a FURBS over any other investment?

- The employer wants to be seen to be giving additional pension benefits, or top-ups to existing pension schemes.
- The employer may not wish to make contributions to anything else.
- The employee wishes to defer a bonus in a certain investment medium.
- The employer does not have an Employee Benefit Trust (EBT), or the potential tax liability of the EBT payment at a later date suggests that the EBT route is inappropriate.
- The FURB can defer capital gains tax.

However, the employee could equally take the bonus, pay the tax, invest into a VCT that grows tax-free for five years, and then take a tax-free lump sum. In addition, he would have had tax relief going into the VCT investment at 30% on £200,000 in any one tax year. If he invested into an EIS qualifying investment, he could defer a capital gain, invest for 3 years only, and have income tax relief at 20% on an investment up to £500,000. However, the VCT or EIS investment strategy may not be to his liking, or whether the VCT or EIS can realise its investments at the due date and time to pay out may be debatable.

Alternative investments could also be ISAs, Unit Trusts, OEICs and offshore funds with gross roll-up. Self-invested Personal Pension Plans could give a tax-free lump sum and a pension scheme and for small amounts could go into a stakeholder pension scheme (even if you are a member of an occupational pension scheme). However, a FURBS is a generally recognised top-up plan for those above the lifetime allowance or on protection where no further contributions could be made to a pension fund under the rules.

12

Partnership and LLP Pension Schemes

Partners and partnerships, LLPs

Partners and LLP (Limited Liability Partnerships) members and salaried partners are the main elements usually of a professional practice or partnership. Equity Partners may contribute to both a personal pension plan or have an occupational pension scheme, such as a SSAS. A salaried partner is an employee who may have a profit share, but does not share in the liabilities or debts of the partnership and would not have a capital account. The salaried partner can be in an occupational scheme or have his or her own pension fund. This part deals with equity partners only. Where partners are mentioned, include LLP members.

Where partners group themselves together, they could contribute to a small self-administered pension scheme (SSAS). However, there must be twelve or fewer partners to do this. For a larger group, a group personal pension plan is more usual (GPPP). Smaller partnerships may have individual personal pension plans, such as SIPPs or the older retirement annuity plans (Section 226 contracts), similar to the self-employed.

Partnerships in England and Wales and Northern Ireland are not legal persona as they are in Scotland. In the former, it is the individual members of a partnership who are trading and not the partnership itself.

For taxation purposes, however, income tax for the partners throughout the UK is assessed in the name of the partnership. Partners have been directly assessed from 6th April 1994, when joint assessment was abolished.

Partnerships are governed by the partnership agreement. It is common to find a clause stating that individual partners must provide for their own retirement funding, where there is no partnership pension fund in place. Pension funding is the major method of building wealth outside the business and of making contributions from pre-tax profits.

Unfunded partnership pensions

However, a partnership does not have to have a funded pension scheme. The partnership itself can pay a pension (as an annuity under TA 1988 s.

628 and Revenue statements of Practice D12 (10/2002) and SP 1/79) to retiring partners, which has not been pre-funded. Contributions made are tax deductible to the other partners in their partnership proportions. To qualify as earned income for these allowances, the pension (annuity) payable must:

*   be paid in accordance with the partnership agreement or supplementary agreement
*   not exceed 50% of the average profit of the retiring partner for the best three of the last seven years before retirement
*   allow a tax-free cash sum of 25% of the notional accumulated sum to be taken
*   be allowed to increase, and where necessary, be paid to a spouse or dependant
*   be paid direct or by the purchase of an annuity.
*   Life assurance can also be funded.

Such a 'fund' may be used for the benefit of the partnership. No loans are allowed if a fund is established, but the fund can purchase commercial property from the partnership and lease it back on commercial terms.

The unfunded pension scheme of annuity payments means that the retiring partner will not be charged to capital gains tax on the capitalised value of the annuity as long as it is regarded as reasonable recognition for past services to the partnership. A reasonable annuity is calculated by taking an average of the partner's best three years assessable profits shares out of the last seven, and then not exceeding the fraction provided in the table below:

Years of service	Fraction per year
1-5	1/60
6	8/60
7	16/60
8	24/60
9	32/60
10 or more	40/60 or (2/3)

Example

Fred Money has been a partner in the legal firm of Level Head and Money for 20 years. In the last seven years, the best three years assessable profits have been £88,675, £127,320, £56,005. The average is therefore £90,667. The annual gross annuity payable to Fred will be 2/3 x £90,667 = £60,444 (net £60,444 − £12,088 (20%) = £48,356)

There are 5 partners in the firm (other than Fred), who will be paying the annuity, and their share is deducted in calculating their taxable income. They deduct basic rate income tax when making the payment and claim relief at the higher rate through their tax returns. Fred pays tax in the normal way on this annuity income. He has received it net of basic rate tax and may have further tax to pay (or reclaim) depending on his personal tax position.

Each partner has gross £12,088, net (12,088 – £2,417) = £9,671 to pay.

Partners may therefore provide for pensions in a tax efficient way without having to set aside capital, if they have left things too late, or merely prefer this course of action. However, their ability to keep up payments in the future must be measured against saving for retirement income through a proper pension fund, rather than relying on a notional one, as outlined above.

Limitations for the unfunded scheme include problems when profits fluctuate, and possibly lower pensions when there has been no funding.

Where partners pay a pension to a retired partner (taxable as income) the payment is not regarded as deductible in calculating partnership taxable profits. This is because it is regarded as a purchase payment of the retiring partner's share of the partnership. It is better to calculate an annuity to the retiring partner within the allowable capital gains tax limits (taxable in the hands of the recipient and deductible for income tax to the payers). The annuity route is more tax efficient in providing income to a retired partner.

Under the post-A Day rules, you can fund for any amount up to the Lifetime Allowance of £1.8 million in 2010/11 in your year of retirement, notwithstanding the Annual Allowance on contributions.

Details of SSAS, Group Personal Pension Schemes (GPPPs), Personal Pension Plans, and Stakeholder schemes are explained elsewhere and are all applicable for equity partners.

Purchasing property

Whether a SIPP or a SSAS, these pension schemes can be used to purchase commercial property that is then let to the business. Rental income accrues tax-free in the pension fund; the value of the property accumulates tax-free and if sold there is no capital gains tax. After A Day, 6th April 2006, the connecting provisions have been abolished which means the business can purchase the property from a partner. Alternatively, the partner or LLP member can pass the property into the pension scheme(s) as an 'in specie' transfer and receive tax relief for doing that.

Doctors and other qualifying members of the medical profession can contribute to both the NHS pension and to other pension schemes and special rules apply for this.

Salaried partners can be members of their own personal pension plans, or as employees in the partnership scheme for employees, usually a group personal pension plan.

13

Starting a Pension Fund – What to Do Next

As they say, you're never too young to start! With the advent of stakeholder pensions, the starting age had dropped from 18 to less than age one, and you can contribute without relevant earnings and still get tax relief as pension contributions are now made net of basic rate tax.

You don't even need to contribute to the pension fund yourself – someone else can do it for you, and pension savings are now being made by parents as well as grandparents for children and grandchildren, as investments for the future.

Look at this example:

Example

> Jim decides that he will contribute the maximum stakeholder pension for his new son Darius of £3,600 gross (£2,880 net). He makes one payment and this is invested at a projected annual compound return of 8% per annum. In fifty years time, this will be worth £168,845.
>
> Alternatively, Joan, age 30, makes a pension payment of £300 per month for 20 years – she will have a fund, if invested at 8% compound per annum, of £196,408. She wishes to retire at age 50, and has made no pension provision.

The steps in the process for starting a pension are as follows.

1. Decide what level of contribution you can afford to make. Even though you may save tax, do not over-stretch yourself. Once a pension contribution has been made, you cannot access the money until the earliest retirement date.

2. Determine your pension plan status.
   - If employed, and if your employer does have a pension scheme, then you can invest into an AVC/FSAVC route for your contributions, or consider a stakeholder pension scheme, or personal pension plan.

- The new rules allow workers to take flexible retirement, drawing a pension whilst continuing to work. Some employers may have to change their pension fund rules and employment contracts.
- You could continue to pay in to a pension after you stop work, at £3,600 per annum gross (£2,880 net). These payments attract valuable tax reliefs.
- If your employer has no pension scheme, then consider a personal pension plan (or stakeholder if contributing below £300 per month gross).
- If self-employed then consider a personal pension plan and/or stakeholder variant.
- If a company director or partner, an occupational pension scheme may be considered, such as a SSAS; or a personal pension plan, such as a SIPP.

3. Do you have earnings from employment (net relevant earnings), or earnings such as interest or dividends only? Only stakeholder pension schemes can accept earnings from sources other than employment. Otherwise you may need 'net relevant earnings' to qualify. Determine your earnings status for type of fund.

4. Can your employer contribute to your scheme? It's worth asking if you set one up – or can you contribute to your employer's scheme? Determine the extent of who can contribute to your plan and how much.

5. Can you make monthly contributions, or do you have single lump sums to invest? Regular premiums by direct debit ensure that you don't forget to make your contributions. However, it has been cheaper in the past to only make single premium contributions as the charging structure for regular premiums was higher. Nowadays, many product providers have the same charging structure whether a monthly or single premium. Determine whether to make regular premium contributions or single premiums, or perhaps both, depending on your circumstances.

6. Do you want waiver of premium insurance? What this means is that, for regular contributions, you can insure against serious illness or disability where you cannot work, and the insurer pays your pension contribution for you, if this is the case. This is not available on stakeholder, but can be a stand-alone addition, and is not expensive. PHI schemes also cater for pension premiums if disabled. Determine whether to have waiver of premium cover, or not.

7. What is your investment risk profile? Do you want a managed investment fund, or options to select from a bigger range of investment opportunities? Determine how you want your funds invested.

8. Do you want to protect your fund for your heirs and dependants should you die? If employed, you may qualify for death in service benefits, or you may need to insure your own fund. Determine how much life cover you need, and why.

9. Select your normal retirement date. When you take out a pension plan, you would have to choose a date between age 55 and 75.

10. Select a target pension fund to aim for. How much must you save over the years for a financially successful retirement? Use the handy calculator elsewhere in the book.

11. Decide whether to go direct to a pensions' provider or whether to use an intermediary financial adviser to help you with your selection. Be prepared to pay a fee or commission, depending on your preference. Choose your plan, going direct or through a financial adviser.

12. Make sure the plan benefits are written in trust to avoid inheritance tax later if you die, and that beneficiaries are determined.

13. Make sure you keep within HMRC funding limits.

14. Set up your plan and make your contributions, then monitor progress on a regular basis, to see if you can increase contributions in future years.

The above steps will help you with your planning. As with most things in life, you get out what you put in, so accept responsibility for your own planning and don't leave matters to chance. Through each of these steps, there may be research and analysis to be undertaken; however this is done for you if you use a qualified financial adviser in your preparation.

14

Choices at Retirement – Pensions, Annuities, Draw-down, Phased

There will be a number of choices and options to be considered at retirement and indeed prior to retirement. If you are a member of a final salary scheme or occupational pension scheme with defined benefits, then the options are less than they would be than if a fund had been built up under a personal pension plan for example.

If a member of a **defined benefit scheme**, the employer/pension trustees will advise on the election options relating to the taking of tax-free cash and the mode of pension payment.

If a member of **defined contribution scheme**, such as a personal pension scheme, stakeholder, SSAS or group money purchase, then there are a number of distinct options available. Previously, the only choice was to take your tax-free cash and then an annuity. Nowadays, you can take the tax-free cash and defer the annuity for as long as possible – to age 75, when you must take an annuity under present legislation, or what is known as an ASP (Alternatively Secured Pension) – continuing with a form of drawdown, in effect.

The choices include drawing down an income from your fund until retirement date (draw-down), retiring from your pension fund in stages (staggered vesting), deferring a decision (at least to age 75), or taking an annuity. There are also options to insure the fund rather than have the guarantees in the annuities, thus increasing income as well as protecting fund assets. New annuities include those now able to pay surpluses back to your estate on death, as well as open architecture annuities linked to growth investments, such as with profits.

It may be that a number of pension schemes are consolidated at retirement into, say, a SIPP – a self-invested personal pension plan – to give greater flexibility, particularly for draw-down. The benefits of the SIPP route include the flexibility to influence investment decisions, to have flexibility to draw income until annuities have to be taken (currently at age 75, unless going into ASP), within the Government Actuary's limits. Included in any SIPP analysis would be a Section 32 Buyout Bond for comparison purposes.

Options

1) Income could be drawn down until age 75 (age 77 from 2011/12), when an annuity must be purchased (draw-down), or taking out an Alternatively Secured Pension (ASP). The main features of **income draw-down** can be summarised as follows:

- income available from fund
- tax-free cash available immediately
- minimum income withdrawal is nil
- maximum income is constrained
- flexibility to change income each year within limits
- income escalation could be limited
- after age 65 more risky than an annuity, possibly
- investment risk varies according to investment strategy and use of guaranteed funds
- death benefits have three options:
  - return of fund less 35% tax
  - fund balance buys single annuity
  - continue with income withdrawals for 2 years then decide
- all income is taxable as employment income (old Schedule E)
- arrange trusts to avoid IHT
- draw-down requires substantial funds and is relatively uncertain
- could deplete pension fund capital
- could apply draw-down to part of the fund, the balance through staggered vesting or phased withdrawals
- flexibility until (maybe) annuity rates improve
- costs of set-up and administration of a SIPP is inexpensive.

2) Pension income could be phased whereby in each period a segment of the pension is encashed or vested to provide tax-free cash and an annuity. Both then provide income for the year. The SIPP would have to be segmented to provide this option. The main features of this option (**phased encashment and annuity purchases**) can be summarised as follows:

- only use income or capital to meet the need requirements
- segmented remaining balances grow tax-free
- tax-free cash may be taken with each segment
- no minimum income
- income depends on the amount vested
- if too high, it could deplete the fund by age 75
- more flexible than draw-down as the whole fund is not committed
- phased annuities can be bought with escalation allowing a mix and match of income types
- may be risky after age 65 if funds are small – but not in this case

- more volatility is possible if fund values are low and one is forced to encash when unit prices are low – investment strategy will determine investment risk and underlying fund investments
- on death, the full fund could be paid to dependants free of tax
- if the transfer was originally from an occupational scheme, then only 25% is available as cash and the balance must purchase an annuity (or drawdown)
- death benefits are better than draw-down
- very tax efficient as tax-free cash is used for income, tax only being paid on the annuity element
- annuities must be purchased for income (unless drawdown)
- tax-free cash is limited to each encashment period.

3) Annuities can provide a fixed income, which is guaranteed until death. The pension fund is invested in gilts and fixed interest, or perhaps a with-profits annuity, or unit-linked annuity. The fund may provide for a variety of income options, including level income, escalating (at say RPI or 3%), or with profits or unit-linked income (the latter not being certain, but dependant on market conditions). The main features of **annuity purchase** can be summarised as follows:

- compulsory purchase annuities' income is taxable (as it comes from pension funds)
- voluntary purchase annuities' income is partly tax-free (as it comes from cash)
- no specific minimum or maximum income
- could have highest levels of income payable for life with guarantees
- no income flexibility
- escalation of income possible at say 3%, 5% or RPI
- best suited to risk-averse investors
- pension fund must purchase an annuity by age 75, or an ASP
- no investment risk on conventional annuities
- there is risk in with profits or unit-linked annuities (they may not perform)
- death benefits – annuities can be guaranteed for up to 10 years usually
- joint life annuities pay out for two lifetimes
- underlying fund could be lost on death to the life office – depends on the type of annuity
- good health buys an average annuity – poor health a better (impaired) one
- annuities are taxed as income
- voluntary annuities have a tax-free element (as they come from say tax-free cash)
- you can, and should, shop around for the best open-market option annuity.

4) **PIPPA class annuities** where the guarantees are taken out of the annuity itself, and placed on the fund. However, you must be insurable for this option. The main features of this option can be summarised as follows:

- better income options
- full original fund value returned on death, tax-free
- better dependants' benefits
- more flexible options available, e.g. where partner dies before you
- increases in income can be between 20% and up to 100%
- higher income guaranteed for life
- dependants' income partly or wholly tax-free if required
- can pass original pension fund value to heirs tax-free.

5) **Annuities returning capital to your estate** were launched in November 2001, but require a minimum fund value of £250,000, and may carry investment risk as funds may be managed within the annuity.

6) **Variable Annuities**. The Government refuses to liberalise the regime for variable annuity schemes. The maximum annuity rate required under guaranteed annuity definition rules (GAD) remains the same. This effectively prevents increased 'equity type' returns from being developed in products. You will not be able to receive a guaranteed income whilst benefiting from future investment returns.

From the above, it can be seen that there are many different options to be considered. The most common annuity-based option (if there are dependants) is usually a joint and survivor annuity, where a pension is payable for two lifetimes, with guarantees of 5 or 10 years (in case the parties die too soon, the annuity continues paying for the guarantee period), level or escalating income (preferable). This is the worst possible option as there is no flexibility with regard to income (particularly if a partner predeceases you), the whole underlying fund is lost on death to the product provider, and annuity rates are at the lowest levels for over forty years. In addition, although the open market option may provide higher income (on average by 11%), the cost of guarantees within annuities accounts for about 65% of the fund value. Income from this source, although guaranteed, will always be very low compared to other sources.

Conceptually, the PIPPA class plan provides the most flexible alternatives, with highest incomes. The full original fund, or as much of it as is insured for, is returned on death, tax-free, and the highest income levels can be guaranteed. The costs of guarantees drops from around 65% of the fund value per annum to less than 4% of the fund value per annum, thus ensuring better income.

The guarantees are separately provided, and the client will have to be underwritten for health reasons. Poor health means higher guarantee costs, but then also higher annuity levels through being an impaired life.

Income draw-down is possible, as well as phased retirement with the PIPPA class option, giving maximum flexibility. You must take a view as to the future movement of annuity rates and investment returns when making your decision.

For a recent client, through shopping around and using the impaired life underwriting, I was able to increase annuity income in retirement by over 400%! Planning with annuities is important because it means greater income from your capital base.

Income drawdown from your pension fund

At retirement, one of your options is to opt for income draw down. This is usually only feasible on funds above £250,000, however people do it on smaller amounts. Your pension assets provide an income which you can take as taxable income, from retirement (earliest age 55) to age 75. This is known as the USP – unsecured pension. After age 75 (77 from 2011/12) you can continue with draw down on a restricted basis, or if not, you must purchase an annuity with your remaining funds.

Drawdown was introduced to give more flexibility with receiving funds, especially where annuities have been low. Annuities tend to increase with age – the older you are, the higher the annuity. An alternative to draw down where you have growth in the annuity funds is through a with-profits or index-linked annuity (as opposed to growth in your pension funds). You can choose from a range of income options, usually the bonus growth. Prudential, for example has experienced annual bonus rate growth of at least 8% since launch of their product.

How does drawdown work?

A new drawdown calculation is done once a year using the Government Actuary's Department tables (GAD) after age 75 and before that every 5 years. These tables can be found at www.hmrc.gov.uk/pensionschemes/gad-tables.htm and there are separate tables for males and females. The tables give the basic amount of pension that can be received per £1,000 worth of capital. Two criteria are used – gilt index yield and age (in complete years at the point of calculation).

Up to age 75, you can select any level of pension between £0 and 120%. After age 75, the maximum pension is 90% and the minimum is 55% of the actuarially determined annuity rate.

Example

Assume John is age 67 in complete years. He has a pension fund of £100,000. Using the 15-year gilt yield on an assumed date, he finds it is 3.87%. This is rounded down to 3.75%. (the figure is rounded down to the next quarter of a percent).

Applying the tables, for a male age 67, with a yield of 3.75%, each £1,000 of capital will provide an annual pension of £71. (A female the same age would have a rate of £83). His £100,000 will provide a pension of £7,100 per annum. He can elect for an annual drawdown of between £0 and £8,520 per annum (120% x £7,100).

After age 75, using the rate for age 75 and over, which is £95 annual pension per £1,000, his £100,000 will provide a basic pension of £9,500, and he can elect a pension income between £5,225 (55% x £9,500) and £8,550 (90% x £9,500) per annum.

At the time of writing (18 July 2010) the current FTSE 15-year gilt yield is 3.87%. However, as these gilt yield rates are subject to change, you should check the rate in the Financial Times or a website such as www.sharingpensions.co.uk/pension_drawdown.htm when making the calculation.

A drawdown review is every 5 years up to age 75 (but allowed more frequently at the direction of the member), and thereafter annually. Planning is important – if you believe the 15-year gilt yield will rise, delay drawdown until it does – if a fall is expected, go for it now. (the 15 year gilt yield fell from 4.04% on 15th May 2009 to 3.87% on 15th July 2010). As complete years are used to calculate the drawdown, a delay until the next birthday is reached may also be a strategy; if about to reach age 75, carry out a drawdown review just before that age is reached, and take the next year's pension annually in advance, to maximise income before the reduction. Also check out the best annuity rates – you may get a better annuity at age 75 than drawdown income – but you could lose your fund to the annuity provider on death.

There are three main changes relating to drawdown flexibility.

Value protected annuities

These provide a regular stream of income in retirement, using a lump sum investment. In the event of death, the value of the initial lump sum is returned, net of any payments that have been taken. The balance is then taxed at 35% – unlike a conventional annuity where the whole fund is lost on death.

Unsecured pensions (USP)

Before age 75, pensions may be unsecured. That means not secured by the purchase of an annuity. They are funded by drawing down income (and capital) from the pension fund. Benefits vary from £0 to 120% of the benefits allowable.

A review of the annual maximum withdrawal from USP may be permitted more frequently than every 5 years but only at the direction of the member. The maximum withdrawal requirement review remains at every 5 years. This applies on or after notifications given from 6th December 2006.

Alternatively secured pension (ASP)

After the age of 75, pension benefits may be alternatively secured – not secured by an annuity, and the rate of drawdown reduces to between 55% and 90% of the GAD rates. By opting for drawdown after age 75, the rate of income to be taken will fall below the likely annuity rate.

Section 69 and Schedule 19 of *Finance Act 2007* makes changes to *Finance Act 2004* and the *Inheritance Tax Act 1984* relating to alternatively secured pensions (ASPs). The minimum amount of ASP paid in an 'ASP year' to a member or dependant must be at least 55% of the 'basis amount' for that year (minimum income). If the minimum amount is not paid then this will be a scheme chargeable payment taxed at up to 40% on the difference between the minimum amount and the actual amount paid. The maximum amount of ASP payable rose from 70% to 90%.

2011/12 tax year

Note that the Emergency Budget has pushed USP up to age 77 from age 75 in the 2011/12 tax year. In all likelihood ASP will disappear – this is part of the Government consultation into retiring and being forced to take an annuity or lower GAD income in ASP.

15

Pension Fund Investments

One has a far greater say in the investment strategy and performance of funds under your control, than if an employer or designated fund manager was taking the decisions, or where older pension funds were concerned, when there wasn't very much choice available to you. As a result, pension funds were more often than not invested into managed life office funds, with average or below average returns. Having said that, can you really do better than an experienced fund manager? Some people can, but the vast majority will find it difficult to do so.

Because of the very nature of the pension fund itself, most investment strategies verge on the cautious, and the older you are, and the closer to retirement date you are, the more cautious you become. Since the millennium, from 2000 to 2010, we have seen great stock market volatility, where managed funds or tracker funds saw losses of up to 30% or more. In the last couple of years, the stock market has been moving down, if not sideways, and has been volatile due to conflict, surging oil prices, and US and UK credit and debt crisis. Not many investors can stomach such investment losses, with possibly a few years to go to retirement. It could financially decimate your retirement plans.

Much has to do with the concept of investment risk. The concept has been related to performance or the lack of it on your funds in the past. However, to the retiree, the risk is often of outliving your capital as people retire younger and live longer, rather than the loss of potential investment performance. So, the protection of capital is important, as is its preservation. Pension funds by their nature are conservative investment vehicles, with a mixture of gilts, fixed interest, property and equity investments, as well as cash, making up the bulk of pension fund investments.

One must have a fund investment strategy. This takes into account many different factors and components, and can be changed at any time. One must take into account the risk profile of the pension member(s), their ages, the amount of the contribution made, the size of the fund (larger funds can sustain greater losses than smaller ones), the payouts to be made by the fund in the future (pensions and tax-free lump sums), whether other benefits are to be provided, such as widows' and children's pensions, costs of administration and other factors. Liquidity is a major factor. For example, your pension fund may own the business premises, but at retirement date it must pay you a pension. Must the business premises be sold at that time, and what are the ramifications for doing so?

15. Pension Fund Investments

Modern investment theory is based on the portfolio theory of investment management. This implies the concept of balance. It is a known fact that over a period of time, some investments may have good returns and go up, others may go down in value. Taken together, the balancing should provide a median return as anticipated by the investor. Other theories involve stock picking and charting, as well as the use of derivatives for exceptional returns (and also exceptional falls). Fund managers allow you to move between funds more often at little or no cost, and many pension fund companies invest their funds into better performing vehicles, even with other competing fund managers to obtain superior performance for their clients.

The past few years have seen greater individualisation and diversification amongst pension fund investors, with the advent of the SIPP, the self-invested personal pension plan, for example. Here, the pension fund contributor can select his or her own investments, from a wide range of choices, including individual share selections. Shares from share schemes can even be used as the contribution to the pension fund if required, and qualify for tax reliefs.

Your choices are broadly as follows:

- choose your own funds and investments
- choose a fund manager to make the decisions
- select a managed fund
- select various investment options, usually from managed, with profits, unit linked, special opportunities, UK equities, global equities, cash, gilts, fixed interest, property and others
- choose a fund supermarket to select a range of investment options in unit and investment trusts, OEICS, and other collective schemes
- allow the pension fund manager discretion to choose the funds to be invested in, according to the risk profile, amount of funds available, size of fund, length to retirement, liquidity and other factors.

It is ultimately your individual choice, because you may not wish to go with a poor performing pension fund product provider, even if you do not personally select the funds. Business owners may opt for a SSAS with wider investment powers, including making loans to the business to purchase capital equipment and machinery, the ability to purchase business premises and other flexible options; or a SIPP to purchase commercial property and hold certain shares. Larger defined benefit and contribution pension schemes will also have a defined investment policy, but this is usually influenced by the trustees of the fund and the employer. A recent case involved a fund manager being sued for not performing as they said they would (Unilever vs Mercury Asset Management), so fund managers are under great pressure to perform. The same is true for trustees of pension funds – they could be held personally liable for not carrying out their functions properly.

However, it must be borne in mind that the client accepts a certain investment mix and strategy and often dictates it, and when there is then failure to perform, one can hardly blame the fund manager.

Where individual pension scheme investors are concerned, their risk profile for investment risk must be taken into account. This profile will also change over time, usually becoming more conservative. A fund with a long investment time frame may be more adventurous early on, but within two years of retirement, should be more concerned with protecting and conserving retirement capital, with a more cautious approach adopted.

It is not only pension funds that have an investment strategy need requirement, for annuities are today more flexible, some being unit- linked, others with-profits, and others having an investment mix. This is because like any growth versus fixed interest investments, the likelihood of being ahead over longer terms usually lies with growth investments. Annuities entirely dependent on gilt or fixed interest portfolios will be slow growers, and will merely produce overall falling future incomes. It is for this reason that in a sustained low interest rate environment, the challenge is in how to squeeze more income out of annuities, the investment vehicles for retirement income, or income drawdown, if that is selected.

Trends in investment portfolio construction are also changing as people are living longer and want to pass their pension funds on to their beneficiaries. The traditional lifetime model of portfolio construction is concerned with the fact that the older the individual, the larger should be the proportion of assets invested in fixed income and cash. However, these investments fail to deliver meaningful returns, especially for income in drawdown and this coupled with planning for maximising pension funds as opposed to a focus on life expectancy has provided more of an emphasis for strategic asset allocation and management. There is now a goal to preserve assets for future generations, and with that the thinking for investments and what they must do has also changed.

Retirement and Life Expectancy

	1981	2008	2050
Male age 65	79	84	87
Female age 65	83	87	89

Those are average figures – the Queen is sending telegrams (an anachronism!) to 100-year olds in far greater numbers than even ten years ago.

There is a danger then that your funds underperform because you allow them to underperform, whereas strategic asset allocation and tactical planning may significantly increase your fund's value.

Investment returns on death is also an important feature. Some pension funds only return premiums paid plus interest at say 4% or 5%, whereas a return of fund is preferred, as it may be higher. A recent client example, where a single premium investment was made into a retirement annuity fund 16 years ago, showed a current fund value of £33,456, whereas the return of premiums plus 4% was £2,367, a significant difference. One can ask the life office to change its terms for a small fee. After all, why should your heirs or estate lose the growth on your funds to the product provider if you pass away? The same argument holds for the loss of the underlying annuity funds on death – it is iniquitous that the life office keeps such investments – after all they don't just disappear. Times are changing, and these centuries-old practices must also change.

Investment growth does not only apply to the build-up of pension funds. If you go into income draw-down after retirement (until age 75 (77 from 2011) when you must purchase an annuity, or go in to ASP), then you also require an investment strategy consistent with providing income, but also for future growth.

Fund management is a highly sophisticated and complex area requiring computer modelling and management where pension fund growth and annuities growth and income provision is required as well as income draw-down. A number of specialist providers offer precisely this type of arrangement when taking out their funds. The fund direction and strategic planning change to suit the individual requirements on a tailor-made basis.

At the actual date of retirement, once you have considered your options, your investments and pension schemes will require decisions to be made to provide you with adequate levels of income and access to capital. If you are investing for income or capital growth, there is a wide range of investments to choose from, depending on your risk profile and the type of investment required. You will also take other factors into account, such as tax efficiency, investment protection, and the investment risk inherent in the investment itself.

At the actual date of retirement, you will have investments already in place, and new investments to be considered for your tax-free lump sums, as well as an investment strategy for your underlying pension schemes if you are deferring a pension to a later date.

The investment process in retirement will be more concerned with ensuring that your retirement income remains adequate and that your investments are properly managed. Ensure that investments do not become obsolete over time and are performing as well as can be expected.

Investment strategies in retirement should take into account the capital preservation of funds, whilst providing an income. A number of product providers now offer income protection within drawdown funds, variable annuity options that give guaranteed income whilst locking in growth in the annuity fund, so that capital does not diminish; and flexibility with regard to phasing income (for example, phasing tax free lump sum payments on a regular basis along with drawdown income for greater tax efficiency). The opportunity to have guaranteed income from a fund when investment markets are under-performing, is to be considered. Some pension funds invest internally into term annuities with income guarantees to provide regular or flexible income (as your circumstances change), but within GAD limits. They are classed as fund investments. These are not the same as compulsory purchase annuities, when your pension pot buys an annuity for life. These variable annuity options have been classed as the 'Third Wave', and the concept has been introduced from the USA (Lincoln, Metlife and Hartford [this latter company has withdrawn from the UK marketplace in 2009]), and is now being taken up by indigenous life offices (Aegon, Standard Life) as well. The guarantees for chosen income levels come at a cost, but if underlying performance of the investment funds is satisfactory, then the retiree has certainty as well as safety, which is a small price to pay, if successful.

Other innovations in the retirement investment field include the ability for an individual to transfer his funds to a scheme pension, which allows a much higher level of income to be taken unrestricted by GAD rates. Income is based on your circumstances, such as mortality and attitude to risk, and income can be managed at higher levels leaving a minimal fund on death – for those who don't wish to lose funds to excess taxation in ASP, a scheme pension could be the answer. The leaders in this field are Hornbuckle Mitchell with their FIPP.

Be prepared to regularly review your investments in retirement and change your investment strategy if your circumstances change. This could be to develop a strategy not to lose investment value because of inheritance taxes, as well as to provide for long-term care, as an eventuality.

When heirs and dependants inherit from you, the process of investment and the investment cycle will begin anew. Younger people with a long time span to go to retirement will invest your older money for adventurous growth, and take risks with it, totally contrary to what you had done over the past ten to twenty years.

16

The Cost of Delay in Taking Out a Pension Scheme

One must begin the pension funding process as soon as possible to avoid the cost of delay. With long-term funding plans, the sooner you begin, the lighter the monthly investment load or burden to be undertaken. The cost of delay is the loss or reduction of final fund benefits (what could have been, had you started earlier), and what that might mean to you, in terms of reduced income.

By examining the table below, you will see the impact at various ages on the eventual fund value, by delaying by only one year the beginning of your investment funding plan.

Cost of delay – eventual fund value lost by delaying further provision by only one year at different ages. Assume that the retirement date is age 65.

Delay period	% loss of benefit – retire at age 65
from age 21 to 22	10%
from age 31 to 32	15%
from age 41 to 42	16%
from age 51 to 52	18%
from age 61 to 62	38%

As you can see, by merely delaying the beginning of the funding of your investment plan by one year, at various periods in your life, a significant negative impact is made on your eventual fund value. The impact is much higher, the longer you delay.

Example

Fanny has decided at age 21 to delay the funding of her pension fund by one year. She was going to invest £1,000 a year into pension funding. That £1,000 delay will cost Fanny 10% of the value of her final pension fund at age 65. To prove it, take £1,000 and invest it at, say, 10% compound interest for 44 years and also 43 years. At a term of 43 years: £60,240 is the fund value. At a term of 44 years, the fund is worth £66,265, a difference of £6,024, or 10% more. That 10% of fund could buy you an income for life, which you now won't have. Think about it.

The target funding figures should also adjust. For example, because you didn't fund £1,000 at age 21, you should have to now fund more than £1,000 at age 22 to make up the difference, if you want the same end fund benefit. That is why at age 61, the difference is 38%, because the loss of a year when so close to age 65 means considerable funding is required because of the delay by one year, and the ground that has to be made up.

So, don't delay, act right away! A parent or grandparent investing £3,600 gross (£2,880 net) just once when the child is a baby and leaving that to compound over the next 55 years at 7% will be £165,970, whereas investing £234 net per month from birth to age 60, growing at 7% with a 1% charge pa, would have a pension fund value of £1.87 million. If you ceased payments into the fund at age 18, it would compound to £1.26 million.

17

Pension Rights

The past decade has seen a surge in pensions' legislation largely resulting from European directives, but also from appellate division cases and cases heard at the European Courts of Justice and Human Rights at Strasbourg.

There has also been greater awareness and protections offered with regard to pensions schemes, as a result of the fraud perpetrated by Robert Maxwell on the Mirror and other pension funds, the pensions mis-selling debacle of the late eighties and early nineties, where people were transferred from perfectly good final salary schemes into personal pension arrangements, and now companies having to reflect final salary schemes on their balance sheets – something that could affect their profits, if the scheme is not properly funded.

Pension scheme liabilities are such that trustees could be held personally responsible with unlimited liability and directors of company pension schemes could go to gaol if schemes are not properly and adequately funded.

Sexual equality is ensured since the Barber v Guardian Royal Exchange case in 1990 requires men and women to receive equal pay for equal work and defines pay as including a benefit from a company pension scheme. Mr Barber could now receive a redundancy benefit similar to that a woman might receive (he was getting less) in the same situation. However, this is only applicable to post-1990 schemes and other cases followed to bring about sexual equality in pension schemes. This means no discrimination on differing pension ages, and equality of pension provision for men and women. Occupational pension schemes must give equal access to benefits as well as equal benefits, and this is now proving to also be the case for part-timers.

In the European case of Bilka-Kaufhaus in 1986 it was found that employees could not be excluded from an occupational pension scheme if that discrimination was indirect and on the grounds of being a part-time worker. Part-timers can demand to belong to a pension scheme, so long as they pay their share of the pension contributions, and admission to the scheme can be back-dated to 1976. These actions have clarified the rights of workers, but will be costly for employers, especially those with large part-time work forces.

Since 6th April 1988, employees have the right not to join an employer's pension scheme or to remain members of it. If they do leave, they are under no obligation to join any other scheme and the employer does not have to contribute to it if they do so.

Employee members must have pension scheme information disclosed to them, which includes an annual report and actuarial valuation. This will change with employee compulsion and auto enrolment (NEST) being mooted for 2012 (although an employee will still have the right to opt out).

Whilst almost all of the case law and legislation has been around occupational pension schemes, the principles have been taken on board for all other pension arrangements with regard to equality of benefits, and no sexual discrimination on pension benefits. So much so, that it looks like unisex annuity rates are becoming more common, which will probably mean lower annuity rates in the future, as females are usually rated down because they live five years longer than men, on average.

It has also spawned new pensions instruments, such as the stakeholder pension, the first of many to meet the CAT standard kitemark on costs and transparency with regard to values and charging structures. For example, there is a 1% charging structure limit. That means real value for money for pension policy owners, hitherto with vastly decreased values due to charges and commissions. Already the filtering process has begun with some product providers adopting the processes across other products, and enabling fees to be charged for work done for clients as opposed to high commissions. As far as pension rights are concerned, one can now insist on better values and receive better products. The complaints procedures are quick to address or redress situations where there has been mis-selling or other misdemeanours, and pensions law and practice is very tightly regulated and controlled now.

We have tight compliance on the one hand, but an opening up of individual investment opportunity on the other, with the new 'defined contribution regime' allowing members to enjoy the benefits of defined contribution schemes (like stakeholder pensions), whilst also experiencing the benefits from a defined benefits scheme (like an occupational final salary scheme). The advent of A Day has meant that many of the old restrictions have gone, and these include:

- restrictions on employees earning over £30,000 having second pension arrangements, like stakeholder – now anyone can invest up to 100% of salary capped at £255,000 in 2010/11 (subject to special provisions for those earning over £150,000 p.a. – see Chapter 4).
- changing pension plans more easily – employees with limited option AVC/FSAVCs can change to personal pension plans, like SIPPs.
- taking cash free cash from AVCs and protected rights funds is now possible
- restrictions on fund investments have been lifted – some remain for SSAS and SIPPs, for example personal investments such as fine wines and holiday homes, but the spectrum overall is broader
- banishment of age discrimination on retiring and carrying on working whilst drawing a pension is now possible

- deferring your state pension for a lump sum later ...

... and a host of other changes with regard to protected rights in funds, the MFR for companies; the pensions protection fund for insolvent schemes, and so on. The Green and White Papers and Turner and other reports have advocated change on a large scale, with modifications to the state pension and S2P, and protection of the pensions rights of workers, such as carers.

There are further protections offered within the pension schemes themselves. For example, group money purchase and personal pension schemes that have contracted out under the Social Security Act 1986 will have protected rights separately identified to ensure that the corresponding fund is used to purchase prescribed benefits at age 60. (Even tax-free cash is allowable now from protected rights funds.)

One area that has vexed pension scheme members in the past has been in relation to bankruptcy and the protection offered to pension benefits. The general rule is that occupational pension schemes are safe and their assets cannot be attached. Personal pension schemes may be a different matter. Usually if aged over 55 from 2010, the trustee in bankruptcy has forced retirement to attach the tax-free lump sum, as well as the pension payments that flow from the fund. Pension assets could also be attached if contributions had been made in fraud of creditors.

Where pension rights are concerned, you have the right to belong to a scheme or not, to make contributions as best you can, and to be treated fairly and equally, both as a worker and also as a member of a pension scheme. It is your right to take up a pension scheme, and to contribute to it, even if you have no relevant earnings, and are a babe in arms. You have the right to make representations to pension fund trustees and to receive certain reports and accounts and to question how a scheme is being run or even invested. Some of the rights are common law ones, others flow from case law and statute. You have the right to have your pension fund protected from others, including your employer and unscrupulous salespeople who may have misadvised you to your detriment, and you may even have a right to compensation if you have lost value or pension benefits.

Post-A Day protection of pension rights

Individuals can protect the pension rights they have accrued up to A Day, if these would have been greater under the old rules. Some protections are automatic, others require action from you. You should keep detailed pension and earnings records of pre-A Day entitlements (before 6th April 2006). The rights to protect are under the Lifetime Allowance, and from the lifetime allowance charge – the tax on benefits if you exceeded the Lifetime Allowance when benefits are taken. The excess is taxed at 25% if a pension is taken and at 55% if a lump sum is taken. These protections are known as primary and enhanced protection and are covered elsewhere.

If your right to tax-free cash is more than 25% and you are in an occupational pension scheme, this will be automatically protected even if you do not need to claim protection from the lifetime allowance charge. However, other conditions may arise and you may need to check the position to ensure the fund and tax-free cash are protected.

18

Pension Transfers and Opt-Outs

If you are moving jobs, you may have to transfer from an existing pension scheme with your old employer to the new employer's pension scheme, or set up your own scheme if you become self-employed. You may even decide that pension schemes are not for you and wish to opt out of your current employer's scheme, or think you can do better by setting up your own pension fund. Some people may not like the 'lock-in' nature of pension schemes and try to transfer their funds to another country or pensions regime where maybe they can enjoy better cash benefits. There are many reasons for wanting to transfer pension benefits or to opt out of their present arrangements, and some of these aspects are covered below. Comment was made in a previous chapter with regard to opting out, and this chapter focuses on the various reasons for making a transfer from one fund to another.

Transferring from one employer to another

The pension fund trustees and administrators must give you a transfer value. This is usually less than the current value of the pension scheme, but some schemes offer the current fund value to transfer. Others charge a penalty to move funds.

If moving jobs, then you have the choice of leaving your pension benefits and funds where they are and making them 'paid up'. At retirement date, you will then enjoy reduced benefits for your service to the time of leaving.

If leaving an occupational pension scheme, then you should receive a 'leaving service benefits statement' that must be produced within two months of leaving. This will give you various options.

You would have the option of a refund of contributions made. If you leave with less than two years' qualifying service, a refund of your own contributions may be made (but not the employer's), with 20% tax deducted from the payment made.

If you leave without the refund of contributions, then your benefits are preserved in the occupational pension scheme, unless you wish to transfer a value to another fund. Preserved benefits are usually paid out as a deferred pension at normal retirement date, based on your years' service to date of leaving. If you left after 1st January 1991, the deferred pension will

111

be revalued on the basis of the lower of the RPI or 5% per annum compound up to the year before normal retirement date.

If you were a member of a money purchase (defined contribution) scheme, then the investment yield or bonuses must accrue and be applied at the same rate as existing members would have, towards your final benefits.

If you have left your employer after 1st January 1986, then if entitled to preserved benefits, you would acquire a right to a cash equivalent which is called the transfer value.

This must be used as follows:

- to buy additional rights in another approved occupational pension scheme
- a single premium transfer to a section 32 buy-out policy to buy a policy from another pension provider
- a single premium to a personal pension scheme or a stakeholder pensions scheme from another pension provider.

A transfer value analysis should enable you to make decisions as to the best possible option for you. If you left the fund with the old employer, a major consideration is whether that scheme would offer pension increases to you. Also, if it was a contracted out pension scheme (contracted out of SERPS or S2P), then there would have been a need to provide for a GMP (guaranteed minimum pension) under a section 32 policy, or to provide for protected rights under a personal pension scheme.

If you were a member of a personal occupational pension scheme, such as an EPP (Executive Pension Plan), as opposed to a grouped occupational scheme, then it may be possible to transfer the scheme to a new employer, but new HMRC approval is required, and note that the new employer does not have to take it on. There may also be issues with years' service in working out the benefits, but this is usually treated as continuous.

Transferring from an employer to a self-employed scheme

The same options and considerations need to be taken into account as above. However, as a self-employed individual, you may only have a personal pension plan or a stakeholder plan. There is no problem in transferring fund values from an occupational pension scheme to a personal pension plan, but note the comments on the possibility of having to provide for a GMP through a section 32 buy-out contract rather than a personal pension plan. You would have to analyse the position carefully and take all factors into account. You could leave the scheme where it is, or make the transfer.

Pension transfers and opt-outs are complicated issues, and professional advice may be required before acting.

It is important to bear in mind that transfers of benefits in respect of A Day service, which take place after A Day, may result in the loss of certain pre-A Day protection.

The tax-free cash sum, for example, may have been protected at 1.5 times final pensionable salary in the transferring scheme, which would then need to be tested against the 25% overall cash limit of £450,000 for 2010/11.

Transfers from a retirement annuity contract

Consider the importance of guaranteed annuity rates, if there are any – a client could get a bigger annuity than the open market option offers. Guaranteed annuity rates are no longer used to calculate tax-free cash from an annuity. The tax-free cash will be 25% of the annuity fund value.

Also consider death benefits. Many retirement annuities only offer a return of contributions, with or without interest. Some may offer a return of fund. Other registered pension schemes offer a return of fund as standard.

Transfers from a free-standing AVC

Check that the scheme rules have been amended to allow for 25% of the fund as tax-free cash – if not, then consider moving to a fund that does offer this. Under the new regime there is now no link between benefits from an AVC/FSAVC, making transfer options more flexible.

Transfers and Section 32 buy-out policies

Whilst the original reasons for using a section 32 contract may have been appropriate, after A Day they may not be. A Section 32 takes transfers from occupational pension schemes. There is a protection of the GMP (Guaranteed minimum pension). The cost of providing the GMP is increasing and is actually paid from the non-GMP fund of the member. So, the member's fund covers the guarantee. It is only when the member's non-GMP fund is used up that the product provider covers the deficit, if any.

There is no tax-free cash available from the GMP. If you did transfer to another fund, any protected tax-free cash greater than 25% for non-GMP funds will be lost on transfer. You can take pension benefits from age 55 that includes protected rights. GMP is not normally available until state retirement age (60 for women, 65 for men, but rising); You can take pension benefits early from a section 32 policy with GMP, but the GMP portion is only available from state pension age.

Death benefits also differ under a section 32 policy and other pension schemes. These are that the funds must first be used to provide for a spouse/civil partner's GMP; then a spouse/civil partner's pension with post-97 funds. Any balance can be used to provide a lump sum. Under a defined contribution (DC) scheme, the protected rights element would be used to purchase a 50% spouse pension, and the balance could pay out a lump sum.

Section 32 policies have a narrow investment range, because the GMP requires a low risk fund. Protected Rights can be invested in a wide range of insured funds. A transfer could offer a wider range of funds and therefore higher potential benefits.

Transfer reviews

If considering transferring to another pension scheme, make the following checks:

- Consider the charges under the contract.
- Are there penalties on leaving one plan for another?
- How competitive are charges between different product providers?
- Consider the investment options available.
- Consider the benefit options available- does the product offer ASP and USP options as standard?

Transfers at retirement date

Retirement is a time of consolidation of pension funds and the implementation of options. It is possible to transfer from an occupational pension scheme to a personal pension scheme before retirement and then to retire from the latter. The reasons for doing so may include better pension benefits, particularly if medically impaired and much higher annuity rates are available than the occupational pension scheme which does not take these factors into account (being purely a mechanical process based on years' service and final salary).

In addition, you may get better death benefits as well as dependants' benefits through making the transfer. Occupational schemes usually don't pay benefits to anyone other than a widow or widower, so a divorced ex-spouse whom you wish to benefit may not benefit, or another third party. By moving your scheme in this way, on your death, other parties may benefit.

You may also wish to consolidate your retirement annuity funds. Income draw-down does not apply to retirement annuities, so a transfer to a personal pension scheme of the retirement annuity funds would facilitate this. Similarly with using the open market option – a transfer must first be made to a personal pension plan to do this. Significant higher annuity benefits may be achieved through the open market option, but also higher rates may be offered for larger funds being placed with annuity providers.

The same applies to a consolidation of personal pension plans to mature at the same age if required or for better deals, impaired life quotes and annuity purchase. Bear in mind though that some retirement annuities and personal pension plans may have high level annuity guarantees and perhaps one would get a better deal by staying with the existing product provider than using the open market option, and the situation needs to be carefully analysed in each case.

Transfers may also be in the client's interests to achieve higher death benefits, especially where the death benefits are a return of premiums plus, say, 4% as opposed to a return of fund. Watch, however, the effect on contribution funding and the value of tax-free cash levels, especially with retirement annuities with longer than average terms.

Early retirement

If you wish to retire earlier than normal retirement date, and are in an occupational pension scheme, then a penalty factor will be applied, the amount of which depends on the rules of your pension fund. You could be better off by making a fund transfer first, rather than by retiring early from an existing occupational scheme.

Early leavers

The new position is that after April 2006, you will have a right to a refund of contributions, but after three months' membership of a scheme (as opposed to two years for most schemes previously and only your contributions), the employer's contributions may now also be taken, when transferring to a new arrangement.

'Winding up' lump sums

The change requires conditions to be met only by the current employer, not any previous employers at the time the winding-up lump sum is paid, and applies after 6th April 2006.

19

A Pension for Your Spouse and Family Members

There are a number of different pension options when considering how to provide a pension for one's spouse or civil partner or partner or family members.

Using your spouse or partner in the business can save you thousands of pounds, but also help by boosting retirement and pension funding significantly. Ensure that your spouse has an employment contract if an employee, or is included in the partnership agreement, if a partner.

Salaries paid to partners or spouses are tax deductible, and, at lower limits, no national insurance contributions are payable. The first £6,475 as the personal allowance in 2010/11 (or £9,490 if aged 65-74, or £9,640 if aged 75 or over) is not taxable, and by creating another taxpayer with lower tax rates, can save money all around. It also helps to get the housekeeping tax deductible!

Pension planning should involve the family unit and not be the sole preserve of perhaps one partner only. There is tremendous scope for pension contributions by the business as well as individually.

Firstly, the introduction of the Stakeholder pension scheme has opened a number of doors, in that no 'net relevant earnings' are required. Anyone, as well as the employer, can contribute to a stakeholder pension for a spouse or family member. The maximum annual contribution is £3,600 gross with a net payment of £2,880 being made (net of the 20% rate of basic rate tax).

At retirement date, which must be between ages 55 and 75, a tax-free lump sum of 25% of the fund can be taken and a reduced pension, or a larger pension and no tax-free cash. The pension or annuity is taxable. Or the funds can be used for income draw down.

If the spouse or partner has earnings, then a contribution can be made of 100% of earnings up to £255,000 in 2010/11 to pension plans. With lower earnings or no earnings, you can still contribute £3,600 (£2,880 net).

The contribution made is tax relievable and no NIC is payable on pension contributions. The treatment at retirement is similar to stakeholder pensions mentioned above.

If the spouse or partner is employed, then an Executive Pension Plan (EPP) can be offered with single premiums payable, or monthly regular contributions, or a combination of both. Funding limits are generous, and actuarially based on age, years to retirement and salary. The following example shows this.

Married male or female retiring at age 60, salary £3,432 per annum

Present age	Annual Current Funding	as a % of salary
25	£892	26%
40	£1,750	51%
50	£3,809	111%
55	£7,928	231%

The level of earnings as an employee is below the national insurance level (in 2010/11, this is £5,720.52 p.a. or £110.01 per week), and no income tax is payable, because the earnings are below the personal allowances level, which is £6,475. The business can pension these tax-free earnings, at a substantial level. The contributions paid by the business are tax deductible. At retirement date, the normal rules for an occupational pension scheme apply.

Your spouse or partner could become a partner in your business, and make contributions to a personal pension scheme, or be a member of an occupational scheme such as a SSAS, where the business contributes for him or her. Obviously, income or profit share must be proven to participate.

You may even have a combination of schemes and arrangements. For example, you may have the stakeholder and also the EPP.

There are many different ways to ensure that your spouse or partner, and indeed other family members, benefit from having their own pension funding and the financial security that comes with it. It is also beneficial in that the housekeeping, usually paid out of after tax income, can be made into a tax-deductible item, and can provide a firm basis for pension funding.

Important also is the fact that retirement planning encompasses all family members who can contribute to it. This ultimately lessens the strain for the main breadwinner, and provides financial independence for the other parties.

It is now possible to have a 'family SIPP or SSAS' to pass residual pension funds on to family members (or anyone else) on death. The scheme must be with the same pensions provider. There are no tax charges if used by a surviving spouse or partner, but funds passing after that are subject to tax and this includes inheritance tax and scheme sanction charges. Family pensions' arrangements are covered elsewhere in this book.

A parent or grandparent can also contribute to a pension scheme for a child (there is no age restriction), and sizable pension funds can be built up – a guaranteed return is offered by HMRC through tax reliefs of up to 40%/50% of your contribution.

20

Tax Implications of Pension Schemes

The general rules are as follows, for pension schemes, pensions, annuities, and tax-free lump sums. For rules governing contributions by high earners (those earning over £150,000 pa), see Chapter 4 and other sections.

Contributions

Contributions to the pension scheme are tax relievable within HMRC limits. The level of contributions and tax relief is determined by the type of pension scheme you have, your age, sex, income that qualifies, whether the scheme is a personal one or owned by the employer; actuarial determinations and investment performance affect future funding on some schemes; costs are also a major factor.

Contributions by an employer to a registered pension fund on behalf of an employee or ex-employee will be allowed as a deduction against taxable profits, provided they are deemed to be 'wholly and exclusively' for the purposes of an employer's trade. Ultimately what the employer can contribute is undefined and at the discretion of the local inspector of taxes.

Occupational pension schemes (owned by the employer)

- **Defined benefits schemes** – contributions are set by the actuary.
- **Defined contribution schemes** – contributions are determined by the employer, ultimately, with the advice of the actuary.

Contributions reduce the employer's taxable income.
There is no national insurance payable on contributions.
Employee contributions to occupational schemes and individual pension plans are limited to 100% of salary up to £255,000 in the 2010/11 tax year.
Employer contributions may be paid that are greater than the employee's 100% of relevant UK earnings and be tax relievable at the revenue inspector's discretion. However, where the total of tax relievable personal contributions and employer contributions in any tax year exceeds the annual allowance, the employee will be liable for a tax charge at 40% on the excess.

Personal pension schemes (owned by the individual)

Personal pension schemes – you may contribute up to £255,000, but limited to 100% of earnings (taxable profits). Up to £3,600 gross (£2,880 net) may be contributed irrespective of earnings.

Stakeholder pension scheme contributions need not be based on 'net relevant earnings' and £300 per month or £3,600 p.a. gross can be made. Contributions are always made net (£2,880) of basic rate tax.

Contributions to approved exempt pension schemes are tax deductible, either individually, corporately or both.

Individuals at the age allowance trap, where age-related allowances are progressively withdrawn from age 65 onwards where income exceeds £22,900 in 2010/11, can make a personal contribution to a 'relief at source' arrangement and claim a reduction to their total income for the purposes of assessing age-related allowances equivalent to the gross amount of the contribution. The deductible pension contribution can reduce the high effective marginal rate of tax payable on income over the threshold.

Confirmation of previous budgets that from 2011/12 tax relief on pension contributions for individuals with income over £150,000 will be gradually tapered. At £180,000 you will only receive basic rate relief (20%) on contributions. Total income is before deduction for pension contributions and charitable donations. If your income is £130,000 and over and together with your employer pension contributions takes you to £150,000 or over, your pension tax reliefs will be tapered. Anti-forestalling measures came into effect for 2009/10 and 2010/11 to prevent pension contribution increases before the new rules came into effect. The special annual allowance of £20,000 - £30,000 (depending on your circumstances) should cease to apply *after* the 2010/11 tax year (as the tapered pension relief rates come in then).

In specie contributions

Contributions can be made to a SIPP or SSAS in property or assets, and need not be in money. The contribution is made net of basic rate and additional tax is reclaimed for higher rate taxpayers. Be aware though that you may have capital gains tax to pay and stamp duty if making such a transfer. The connecting provisions have been abolished and you can contribute your own commercial property to your pension scheme. The value to be transferred must be within your annual allowance and earnings profile – if not you can make the transfer over a number of years.

FURBS

Contributions made to an unapproved pension scheme, such as a FURB are also deductible to the company, but now only when the benefits are taken. Contributions are now not taxed in the hands of the individual, but the fund will be taxed in his hands. This is the position for post A Day FURBS.

For pre-A Day FURBS, contributions were immediately deductible, but taxed on the employee, and the fund proceeds were tax-free. Up to A-Day there are transitional arrangements, with the pre A Day portion at the old rules and the post A Day portion at the new rules.

See also 'FURBS – tax-free lump cash' in the 'Tax-free lump sums' section below (page 121).

Pensions and annuity payments

Pension and annuity payments from compulsory purchase pension funds are taxable in the hands of the recipient. Drawdown income is also taxable. Retirement annuity contributions are paid gross, with tax relief being obtained via self assessment or claim. This is likely to change in the future to bring contributions into the net of tax basis, as with personal pension plans.

State pension payments

These are taxable in the hands of the recipient. Lump sums payable from the state scheme as a result of deferral are also taxable. However, they are not added to your income to be taxed at increased marginal rates – rather the tax rate of your usual tax liability applies to the lump sum. You need not take the lump sum – you can take an increased state pension instead.

Tax-free lump sums (pension commencement lump sums)

A proportion of the pension fund may be commuted as a tax-free cash lump sum payment.

For personal pension schemes and stakeholder plans, 25% of the fund is tax-free. Pensions cap limits previously applied as to the maximum, but these have now been abolished.

For retirement annuities, the tax-free lump sum is a calculation made as 3 times the annual pension before commutation. Pensions cap limits do not apply.

For retirement annuities transferred to personal pension plans for the open market option, the tax-free lump sum is 25% of the fund value.

For any tax-free lump in excess of the 25% of the lifetime allowance £450,000 in 2010/11 that has not been protected pre-A Day, will be subject to an excess fund charge of 55%.

For occupational pension schemes, including SSAS, EPP, defined benefit and defined contribution occupational pension schemes, HMRC rules apply.

Pre-1987 schemes: 1.5 x final remuneration after 20 years service (with many caveats) There is no cash limit (i.e. no pensions cap).

Post-1987 schemes: 2.25 x the initial annual rate of pension before commutation (including the value of AVCs and FSAVCs), or 3/80ths x final salary for each year of service up to a maximum of 40 years service, whichever is the greater. Therefore one cannot have more than 1.5 times final salary as a lump sum.

Tax-free lump sums were limited by the pensions cap which was £105,600 in 2005/06. Thus, 1.5 x £105,600 = £158,400 is the maximum tax-free cash. Post-A Day (6th April 2006), the pensions cap is abolished. However, tax-free lump sums higher than 25% pre-A Day should have protection. After A Day, if not protected and within the lifetime allowance, tax-free lump sums are 25% of the fund.

FURBS – tax-free cash

The whole of a FURBS pays out tax-free cash without limit for pre-A Day FURBS. After A Day, that portion relating to post-A Day funds becomes taxable.

The pension fund itself

The growth within the approved exempt pension fund is not subject to capital gains tax, income tax, or corporation tax. If assets are sold, there is no capital gains tax payable.

FURBS

Pre-A Day tax is payable on investment (savings) at 20% and dividend income at 22.5%. This is because the fund is not approved nor exempt for pre-A Day funds. Post-A Day FURBS are taxed at 42.5% for dividends and 50% the rate for trusts on all other income.

Non-UK residents

A non-UK resident with UK relevant earnings can make personal contributions and receive tax relief on up to 100% of earnings (before A Day this was not possible).

Post age 75 contributions

You can contribute to a pension plan after age 75, but the contributions will not be tax relievable. Most providers will not accept contributions, though (as benefits must be taken after age 75 and no tax-free commencement lump sum is allowable after age 75).

Penalties and surcharges

After A Day, there are penalties and surcharges for exceeding allowable limits. If your funds exceed the lifetime allowance without protection, then if a pension is taken the penalty is 25% on the excess and 55% on an excess lump sum. If non-permitted investments are made (for example a SIPP investing into a holiday cottage), there will be scheme sanction penalties applying to the trustees. This could be in excess of 45%.

If contributions are made by an individual in excess of the annual allowance (100% of earnings capped at £255,000), the excess is liable to a tax penalty of 40% (unless a case can be made for a refund).

Value protected annuity

If death occurs before age 75, a lump sum benefit is payable being the difference between the annuity purchase price and the payments made up to the annuitant's death. The payment will be subject to tax at 35%.

21

Inheritance Tax and Pension Funds

Strategies on how to pass on pension assets to your heirs. Pension funds and trusts. How to insure your pension fund to pass on the whole fund on death, without paying inheritance tax. The pension regime after A-Day and how it affects your pension assets on death. Death benefits and ensuring maximum payouts. Death in service benefits.

Inheritance taxes can apply to pension fund assets under certain circumstances. Usually, though, there are no inheritance taxes payable until such time as assets have passed to a third party after the pensioner's death. This is a most contentious area, and the Government have made many attacks on it and have equally had to backtrack on some of their more outrageous manoeuvres to fill the State coffers with pension money. Unfortunately, the Government has been dipping into pension assets for many years, one of the most contentious areas being Gordon Brown's infamous disallowance of tax credits on dividends accruing to pension schemes. Another recent area of controversy has been the unfair treatment of pension funds arising on death under alternatively secured pensions (ASPs) (see below), where there are not only inheritance taxes that may be payable, but also very high charges applying to funds passing on death.

Savings culture

People save for pensions both to build funds that will provide them with an income in retirement, and also to provide a pension for their spouses or partners once they have died. This can be extended to providing for dependants' pensions, including children and others financially dependant on the breadwinner. So far, so good – that's exactly what pensions are for. However, most pension fund savers are also building assets within a pension fund, not only to save for retirement, but as part of their capital accumulation. They would like to pass their unused pension assets on to future generations as intact as possible. In the savings culture perpetuated by the Government (encouraging people to save for retirement to cover for the inadequacy of State benefits), we do have an apparently generous tax-based savings opportunity to build protected funds for the future. However, when we lift the veil, the reality is that the current pensions savings culture is only designed to provide for one or two generations. Beyond that, the State seems determined to decimate the savings so carefully nurtured by ordinary people.

Surely, if the present generation can provide pension assets not only for their own lifetimes, but also for future generations, it will greatly reduce reliance on State funding and alleviate the stress of future generations having to make their own pension arrangements, for many years into the future. People do have alternatives to taking out a pension: they can fund for retirement through investments, savings, building a business and selling it, and many other diverse means. However, pensions' savings are synonymous with a retirement planning culture, and should be encouraged.

Pension term life assurance

This is another important area of pension planning which has recently been under attack by the Government.

Those saving for a pension fund who may die too soon will, in all likelihood, not leave much of a pension fund for their dependants. It is therefore vital that the pension fund accumulation phase be protected with life assurance. On death, the life assurance pays out a lump sum and provides funds that can be invested for income, so that widows and their dependants, in the main, have an income (and are not dependant on the State.) In the past, one has been able to purchase tax-relievable term-based life assurance that will fulfil this need, where the premiums have been tax relievable in some way.

Over the years this tax relief has ranged from 5% to 100% of the life assurance premiums. Even if you did not have a pension scheme, you could buy tax-relievable life assurance that would provide funds in the event of your death before retirement. Was the State giving a meaningful benefit to assist with the generation of pension funding? Yes it was. The Chancellor saw fit to withdraw this benefit in the November 2006 budget statement, another indication of the fact that those in Government do not understand the fundamentals of retirement provision. It's not the withdrawal of the tax relief that's the point. After all, one can always purchase non-tax-relievable life assurance at any time. It was the message inherent in the withdrawal, that whatever your personal provision for retirement, you are more or less on your own – another reason why proper planning is important. Tax relief on pension term assurance was abolished on 14th December 2006.

Funding for Retirement

There remain strong incentives to fund for retirement, and there are generous contribution reliefs available to those who do so. There will be an element of compulsion for businesses to ensure that employees have the new minimum NEST pension accounts after 2012.

Contributions into pension funds are deductible from taxable income, and even if you are a non-taxpayer, you will benefit from these tax reliefs at the basic rate of rate. Children can have contributions made for them, and their parents (or grandparents, if they are the contributors) can have tax relief. Once the contribution is in the pension fund, it will grow tax free, and when you get to minimum retirement age, which is presently 55, at least 25% can be taken from your fund in tax-free cash (known as the pension commencement lump sum). You don't even have to retire to take your pension benefits. You can take your tax-free cash and defer the taking of your pension until a later date, if in a private scheme. The rules are different for a company-owned defined benefit pension scheme, where the retirement age is usually 60, and you normally have to take your pension when you take your tax-free cash. In 2010/11 an individual can contribute up to £3,600 without reference to earnings or 100% of earnings up to £255,000. An employer can contribute up to £255,000 less employee contributions, subject to the restrictions placed on high earners – see Chapter 4.

Inheritance tax and pension funds

Occupational pension schemes – defined benefit schemes

Benefits received from occupational pension schemes and annuities are free of inheritance tax. These benefits usually cease after the spouse (or civil partner) or dependants die or the benefit period ends, and no funds are available to transfer to third parties.

Defined contribution schemes
including occupational SSAS arrangements

Benefits received on death before retirement are free of inheritance taxes. On death after retirement, but before the age of 75, there are exemptions for spouses, civil partners and dependants.

On death after the age of 75, if you have an annuity, this dies with you and there is no inheritance tax payable. If you are in an ASP on death new rules will apply as referred to below (see 'ASP – alternatively secured pension'.)

USP – unsecured pension

If, after retirement and up to the age of 75, you have not taken an annuity and have decided instead to draw income from a pension fund, your pension is known as an unsecured pension (USP) and the 'income drawdown' must comply with specific USP rules in order to preserve the fund's tax reliefs. In particular, from retirement age to the age of 75, the income able to be drawn down is subject to an upper limit of 120% of the actuarially determined annuity rate for someone of that age.

On death, the fund can be passed to a civil partner, spouse or dependant without IHT; it can also be passed to a non-dependant third party, whereupon it will be subject to IHT. See the section "Death after retirement" below for further details.

ASP – alternatively secured pension

From the age of 75 on, if you have not taken an annuity and are not receiving a 'scheme pension' and have decided instead to draw income from a pension fund, your pension is now known as an alternatively secured pension (ASP), and the 'income drawdown' must now comply with ASP rules in order to preserve the fund's tax reliefs. The option to continue drawdown at 75 rather than purchase an annuity was only introduced in 2006, as a special concession to people who had religious objections to annuity purchase. Because the Government regards this option as only a concession, and seeks to encourage the majority of people to take out annuities, ASP rules are more restrictive than the USP rules applying up to the age of 75. In particular, the amount which can be drawn down under ASP rules is now limited to a minimum of 55% and a maximum of 90% of the actuarially determined annuity rate for someone aged 75. This means that most people will be worse off in income terms with an ASP drawdown than they would be with an equivalent annuity. (Note that after the age of 75 it is not possible to take out an annuity with a guarantee, so that any surplus funds on death of the annuitant are retained by the pension product provider – another incentive to take out an annuity before reaching 75 and going into ASP)

As well as limiting the amount which can be drawn down, the Government is also seeking aggressively to restrict the ability to pass on any left-over funds from an ASP on the death of the member. To this end the 2007 budget introduced a penal system of "unauthorised payment charges" of up to 70% on transfers post-death to non-dependants, payable *in addition to* inheritance tax charges.

On death, the fund can be passed to a spouse, civil partner or dependant without payment of either IHT or the afore-mentioned unauthorised payment charges; any other transfers are subject to the double taxation referred to above. See the section "Death after retirement" below for further details.

Note that ASP will become under consultation and the age to take an annuity or ASP moves to age 77 in 2012.

Value protected annuity

If death occurs before the age of 75, a lump sum benefit is payable being the difference between the annuity purchase price and the payments made up to the annuitant's death. The payment will be subject to tax at 35%.

Tax-free cash (pension commencement lump sum)

Once you have the tax-free cash, this will fall into your estate for inheritance tax purposes. Any tax-free cash not used up, for example to pay off debts or a mortgage at retirement, and invested into non-protected IHT investments, will be subject to IHT on your death. An IHT-protected investment could be a discounted gift trust investment bond where the discounted portion is immediately out of your estate, or an investment into an EIS qualifying company or portfolio of companies, where the share value falls out of your estate after two years.

FURBS

A Funded Unapproved Retirement Benefit Scheme (FURBS) is a pension benefit scheme set up by employers for a named individual (or individuals), now more commonly known as an 'employer-financed retirement benefit scheme'. Before A-Day (6th April 2006), funds in a FURB on death were inheritance tax free; after A-Day, these funds fall into your estate for inheritance tax purposes. However, they are apportioned for pre and post A-Day, with pre A-Day funds retaining their tax advantages.

Death before retirement

Should you die 'in service' (in other words, before retirement), then the pension fund rules will usually stipulate what sort of death benefits are payable and when.

You may have a pension fund offered through an employer ('scheme pension'), related to your salary and benefits. Alternatively, you may be in a pension fund set up by yourself, such as a personal pension plan.

Employers may have death-in-service benefits arising from the pension fund itself, or the benefits may be provided by group scheme life assurance. The latter is usually available up to retirement age and then ceases. Group life cover is a multiple of salary, for example two to four times final remuneration, or a fixed amount, and is payable to named beneficiaries or dependants. Payments made by the trustees, for tax reasons, are always discretionary, but a letter of wishes is followed, giving direction for lump sum payments.

If there are no additional group scheme or death-in-service benefits, then on death before retirement there would either be a return of current fund value (the better deal), or a return of contributions paid plus say 4% or 5% (worse than a return of current fund value). The differences can be enormous, especially where single premium contributions have been made – return of contributions can be as much as 80% less than current fund values. One can approach the pension provider and ask for a change in how and what death benefits are payable – some will charge you to make this change. This is more likely to be the situation for your own personal pension plans, but could also be the case with some employer-funded schemes.

Such payments on death before retirement are usually tax-free. Partnership group life schemes provide tax-free benefits on death for all partners from 9th April 2003 (not just for the first-dying, which was the previous position).

Dependants' pensions provided on death before retirement will not count towards the standard lifetime allowance. There is technically no limit on benefits that can be provided for dependants on death before retirement. However, aggregate dependants' pensions should not exceed the value of the member's pension to avoid an 'excess charge'. If a pension is paid there can be no guaranteed periods and no provision for value protection. A spouse and children aged under 23 will automatically qualify, as will civil partners. If an unmarried couple, you must provide proof of financial dependency to receive a dependant's pension.

Return of funds and pension contributions and death-in-service life assurance (including pension term assurance) can be paid tax-free so long as the payments overall are within the standard lifetime allowance (SLA), which is £1.8 million in 2010/11, and escalates each year. Above the SLA, there are tax charges. Where the excess is taken as income, the tax charge is 25%; where taken as a lump sum, the tax charge is 55% (unless funds were protected under your own purchased life annuity (PLA) – i.e. an annuity not from a pension fund but purchased using your free capital – when the higher limits will be paid without penalty).

Death after retirement

Once you have retired, you will be receiving your monthly pension or annuity or income drawdown. Your pension funds will have been invested by the pensions' provider to produce an income, and this is generally known as an annuity or pension income. Unless there is a guarantee operating, the main pension itself will come to an end on your death. However, dependants', spouses' and civil partners' survivor pensions may be payable until their own deaths.

The type of death benefits, if any, will depend on the type of annuity or pension's contract, or other arrangements, such as drawdown, in force at the time.

The most common types are as follows.

Occupational pension schemes

If single, the scheme pension will merely cease. Some schemes have a guaranteed period of payment, and pension payments will continue to the estate of the deceased, or nominated beneficiary or dependant for that period of guaranteed payment.

If married or in a civil partnership, usually a reduced pension is payable to the spouse or civil partner, until his or her death, depending on the scheme rules. 50% widow's or widower's pensions are common, but the range could be from less than that to up to 2/3 of the member's pension.

Personal pension schemes and schemes where annuities are payable

Much depends on the type of the scheme. A scheme with a 'term certain' guarantee will pay out for that term and then cease. For example, if the annuity is payable for two lifetimes, but for a minimum of 10 years, and both annuitants die in, say, year eight, then the annuity continues paying for another two years (to the estate or dependants) before it ceases.

If a single life annuity, then the annuity will cease paying out on the member's death, or after the expiry of any guaranteed period if later.

If a joint and survivor annuity, then on the first death, the annuity continues paying to the survivor (usually a reduced amount) until the death of the survivor, when it ceases – unless within the term certain guarantee period, if there is one attached. If the spouse dies before the member, then on the death of the member, the annuity will cease unless within a term certain guarantee period.

If a single-life nil-guarantee annuity is taken, to achieve the highest level of income option, and the underlying pension fund is insured, then on the death of the annuitant, the annuity itself ceases, but the insurance proceeds are paid out in trust outside of the deceased's estate, free of all taxes. This may then be reinvested for income, or for a voluntary purchase annuity that is more tax efficient.

Income drawdown

Where the pension fund is in income drawdown (a USP if the deceased is under 75, or an ASP if the deceased is 75 or over), there are a number of options for the spouse or inheriting financial dependant:

If under age 75: (new rules will apply from 2012)

1. **A return of fund (cash lump sum) less 35% tax** for USP funds,– there is no inheritance tax payable unless it is left to the estate. The option must be taken up within two years of the deceased passing away. Note that in the case of an ASP (where the deceased was 75 or over) this option is only available if the inheriting dependant is under 75; if the inheriting dependant is 75 or over, they must choose option 2 or 3.

2. The remaining fund buys a **single annuity**

3. The spouse or civil partner can **continue with income drawdown** – under USP rules until the policyholder would have turned 75 years of age, or the dependant's 75th birthday if sooner, and thereafter under

ASP rules (see below). The spouse can elect option 3 for up to two years and still switch to option 1 or 2. After 2 years, options 1 and 2 are no longer available.

On the death of the inheriting dependant, the fund will be subject to IHT in the dependant's estate, and subject to unauthorised payment charges if the drawdown has come within ASP rules (see below).

If there is no spouse or partner, the fund can be passed free of IHT to dependant children under age 23 or other qualifying dependants for continued income drawdown. However, the fund can only be passed *once* free of IHT; neither the spouse nor any inheriting dependant can pass the fund on to subsequent heirs or beneficiaries (a 'second passing') without exposure to IHT.

If there are no dependants, the left-over value of the fund can be passed to a third party, but will be subject to IHT, and also, in the case of ASPs, subject to the unauthorised payment charges referred to above.

If part of the member's investment 'mix' included investing into a short-term annuity, this is not to be confused with a pension annuity. A short-term annuity is an investment that can be made up to age 75 and may not be for more than 5 years. This type of annuity provides a certain flow of income for a short period. On death whilst taking income from this type of annuity, a full refund is payable less the 35% tax charge. No lump sum can be payable from the short-term annuity.

If Over age 75

The retirement planning options are as follows:

1. Continue to take income from the drawdown fund, if in drawdown, but now under the ASP rules, or

2. Purchase an annuity, which can include single or joint and survivor options.

On Death of the member, the options are as follows:

If there are dependants (which may include a spouse or civil partner or financial dependants up to age 23 or beyond depending on the circumstances, such as mental incapacity):

1. Dependants can take an **annuity.** On their deaths, there are no IHT implications as the annuity ceases, or

2. Dependants can **continue with drawdown.** If the dependant is under age 75 then the USP rules apply; if over age 75, the ASP rules apply. There is no lump sum option as under USP if under age 75. An annuity can be taken at any time, if in drawdown.

If there are no dependants:

1. The value of the fund can be left to charity, in which case no IHT or unauthorised payment charges result, or

2. The value of the fund can be transferred to other pension scheme members, in which case severe unauthorised payment and other charges result, as well as IHT.

Rules governing transfer of ASP funds to non-dependants

A 40% IHT liability is payable on the ASP fund on the death of the member's first inheriting dependant, or on the death of the member if there are no qualifying dependants to inherit, and if the amount is over the NRB. Prior to the changes announced in the 2007 Budget the remaining pension fund could have been passed as a transfer lump sum death benefit to other members of the same pension scheme. Product providers consequently marketed the use of family 'SIPPs' or 'SSAS' schemes to pass benefits to other scheme members without further penalty, within the pension scheme. It was possible to have left-over funds paid as a 'transfer lump sum death benefit' refunded to an employer or to use them to provide benefits to a dependant in the pension scheme who is not a spouse, civil partner or financially dependant person.

Following the 2007 Budget, this has changed. The option to use a transfer lump sum payment has been removed from the legislation, and any such transfer payment, except for payments to a charity, would now be an unauthorised one. This would have significantly higher tax charges, as follows:

Inheritance tax

This is payable at 40% as before, subject to nil rate band provisions (see below).

If ASP assets are not paid to the estate, but to another pension scheme member, the IHT charge will take account of any income tax already paid before the IHT charge arises.

Unauthorised payment charge at 40%

The person inheriting the fund must pay an unauthorised payment charge of 40% – *in addition to* any IHT due. This unauthorised payment charge cannot be paid from the pension fund itself, and other sources must be found to pay it.

Unauthorised payment surcharge at up to 15%

If the amounts passed from ASP in any one tax year total more than 25% of the ASP fund value, a surcharge of 15% is added. This must be paid by the person inheriting the fund.

Scheme sanction charge on unauthorised payment

The scheme provider must pay a sanction charge of between 15% and 40% on an unauthorised payment, which is not deductible from the client's pension fund. If the recipient of the unauthorised payment pays all the unauthorised payment charges due from him, the amount payable by the scheme provider is 15%. This provides a maximum possible charge on the unauthorised payment of 70% (40% + 15% + 15%).

Effective tax rate

The effect of the inheritance tax liability plus the additional charges, add up to an effective tax charge of 82% on the remaining capital (including the scheme sanction charge paid by the scheme provider). In fact, most of the remaining capital could be wiped out as the scheme administrator could also be subject to charges as well as costs. Note that if the pension funds are left to a charity then no IHT or unauthorised payment charges arise.

Nil rate band

The new rules state that the nil rate band (£325,000 in 2010/11) will first be applied to the non-ASP part of the estate (i.e. the estate excluding the ASP fund). Any residual amount of NRB left over can then be applied to the ASP fund. Any NRB still unutilised after treatment of the ASP fund can be passed down with the ASP to the inheritor of the fund (to be utilised in their own estates' accounting for IHT on the ASP).

The payment of IHT and unauthorised payment charges is calculated cumulatively – if IHT is paid first, the unauthorised charges are calculated on the ASP fund *net of* IHT paid; similarly, if the unauthorised payment charges are paid first, the IHT is calculated on the ASP fund *net of* unauthorised payment charges made.

The rules also state that the order in which IHT and unauthorised payment charges are paid will not affect the total charges on the fund. In this respect if IHT is paid *before* the unauthorised charges, the NRB applied against will be 'grossed up' by the total unauthorised payment charge rate in order to ensure equal treatment (see the *Example* below). Assuming a total 55% unauthorised payment charge rate (including the surcharge) this means the NRB will be grossed up by a corresponding amount – i.e. divided by (100 − 55) = 45%.

One beneficial effect of these NRB changes is that it opens the door for an estate to be wound up, without having to wait for details of taxable ASP funds and scheme payouts (which may take up to two years). Had the earlier position applied, where IHT was withheld (or having to be paid by a beneficiary) as a first charge, when in fact it may not even be payable as within the NRB, this would have had unfair consequences for the remainder of the estate assets, deprived of a portion of the NRB.

Example

Jim is aged over 75, is in an alternatively secured pension (ASP), and has a fund of £200,000 at his death in the 2007/08 tax year on 1st November 2007. He has no dependants. He wishes to leave his pension fund as a transfer lump sum death benefit payment to the pension fund of his grandchild, Roger, set up as a stakeholder pension plan when Roger was ten years old (Roger is now aged 14). Jim has a total estate of £250,000 excluding the ASP fund, so that £250,000 of his £300,000 NRB (at the time) is used up on this part of the estate. The remaining £50,000 is used in calculating the tax due on the ASP fund. To make matters more complicated, the IHT on the ASP falls due before the unauthorised payment charges, so the £50,000 NRB is grossed up before calculating the IHT payable. The calculations are as follows:

Position on the Fund

Total ASP fund before tax	£200,000
Less grossed-up NRB (£50,000 divided by 45%)	£111,111
	£88,889
IHT at 40% of £88,889	£35,556
Residual estate subject to unauthorised payment Charges (£200,000 – £35,556)	£164,444
Unauthorised payment charge 40% on £164,444	£65,778
Unauthorised payment surcharge 15% on £164,444	£24,667
Total unauthorised payment charges	£90,444
Total charges, including IHT (£90,444 + £35,556)	£126,000

Roger's Position

Receives a pension fund of	£200,000
IHT withholding charge – Roger pays	£35,556
Unauthorised payment charge – Roger pays	£65,778
Unauthorised payment surcharge – Roger pays	£24,667
Balance to Roger's pension fund	£74,000

Scheme provider

Scheme sanction charge at 15% of £164,444	£24,666

Note that if the IHT had fallen due *after* the unauthorised payment charges the total charges payable out of the estate would still have been the same, although the scheme sanction charge would be higher. The calculations are as follows:

Position on the Fund
Total ASP fund before tax   £200,000

Unauthorised payment charge 40%   £80,000
Unauthorised payment surcharge 15%   £30,000
Total unauthorised payment charges   £110,000

Residual estate subject to IHT (£200,000 – £110,000)   £90,000
Less NRB   £50,000
              £40,000

IHT at 40% of £40,000   £16,000

Total charges (£110,000 + £16,000)   £126,000

Scheme provider
Scheme sanction charge at 15% of the value of the
fund net of IHT paid (15% x [£200,000 – £16,000])   £27,600

Many issues need to be considered when dealing with passing ASP funds to the estate of the deceased or another pension member. Problems include the fact that you might not know what fund amount to base the IHT charge on as the unauthorised payment and other charges need only be made up to 18 months after the event. Any transferable nil rate band from a deceased spouse will reduce the IHT payable in the above example.

Planning areas

1. Review pension planning well before the age of 75.

2. Get the best possible annuity options to avoid the ASP charges. Include as many dependants as possible, to prolong income. At least one product provider can provide an option to go to the age of 80 or more before making the annuity decision.

3. Some may prefer the ASP charges, in order to leave something, however small, to their heirs. However, paying 40% on pension funds after the unauthorised payment charge may still severely restrict the amount of the nil rate band available.

4. Use the unsecured pension route (USP) before the age of 75 to take maximum funds out of your pension scheme and to build up alternative IHT-protected funds, or to enable you to gift excess income to children and grandchildren.

5. Possibly plan to leave funds to charity to escape all charges, and reduce IHT liabilities to your estate.

6. If a younger spouse or civil partner, using the USP before the age of 75, could extend the overall pension benefits available, i.e. on death before the age of 75, the spouse has more available options for IHT planning to pay beneficiaries whilst still alive.

7. Contributions could be made to beneficiaries' pension schemes (even those of very young children under the Stakeholder rules) that are tax relievable, and assets could pass in this way to beneficiaries, in a more tax efficient way than if from an ASP fund after the age of 75. Under USP before the age of 75, drawdown income from the unsecured pension fund can be taken at up to 120% of the GAD (Government Actuary) rate; whereas after the age of 75, income must be taken at between 55% and 90% of the GAD income factor applying to a 75-year-old. One can use this higher income under USP to accumulate funds outside of your estate. However, always bear in mind the fact that you should always ensure you have sufficient income in retirement for your needs, before giving it away.

Phased retirement

Many people prefer to take all of their pension benefits at once. Others prefer to take pension income and lump sums as they see fit, and according to their needs.

If the funds have been phased (where pension segments have been taken as the individual requires them), then the position is as follows.

Death before retirement

On death before retirement, the full fund can be paid to dependants free of tax.

If the transfer was originally from a company scheme to say a personal pension scheme, then only up to 25% may be taken as tax-free cash and the balance as income from an annuity or as unsecured income (drawdown income). One of the annuity options may be the purchase of an impaired life annuity, if you qualify through ill-health or being a smoker. This type of annuity is medically underwritten, and could result in a higher income. For example, Mrs Smith has cancer and her life expectancy is shortened. She could qualify for enhanced income of 50-75% higher than a conventional annuity. People with more than one pension fund may wish to stagger the retirement dates to provide income as well as tax free lump sums when they need them. Phased retirement also enables you to take a tax free lump sum from your pension scheme, but to defer the taking of income or an annuity until much later. You therefore have more flexibility with greater options.

There is no difference in how the various pension funds are treated whether you phase your retirement benefits or not. The same rules will still apply.

Death after retirement

It is unlikely that any death-after-retirement life cover benefits will be available from a pension fund or group life scheme, or death in service benefits scheme, unless provided independently by the annuitant.

Payments of lump sum death benefits cease after the age of 75. However, there are circumstances where they may be paid after the age of 75. These are payments to a registered charity, transfer lump sum death benefits, on scheme wind up where the dependant's pension entitlement is deemed to be trivial (less than 1% of the SLA); and where a lump sum is paid under a 5-year guarantee right that existed on 5th April 2006.

In most instances, it would be in the interests of all parties to have death benefits paid in trust outside of the estate, to avoid probate before being paid out to beneficiaries. This means that such death benefits in trust will escape IHT.

Life assurance in trust

The use of life assurance is a powerful inheritance tax planning tool. Life assurance underwritten in trust is free of inheritance tax. It is most useful to provide immediate liquidity in a person's estate, which may require cash to pay inheritance taxes, to fund trusts or to provide an income for dependants, supplanting or supplementing pension or annuity income.

The concept of life assurance can also free up your thinking with regard to increasing your income in retirement – particularly when it comes to the choice of annuity-type. One of the major reasons why people wait until they are as old as possible before taking an annuity is because at younger ages, annuity rates are very low. These annuity rates increase generally rate for age. As a result they get better when you get older. The more guarantees you have with an annuity, such as guaranteed periods, paying an annuity for two lifetimes, taking income in advance, escalating your income – the lower the annuity income – in fact annuity costs can take up over 65% of your annuity income. By reducing the guarantees, and perhaps limiting the annuity to single-life you increase income, but reduce inheritable value; and that's where the life assurance policy comes in.

The best deal for you, in terms of income received during your retirement, would be a single annuity with no guarantees. That will pay you the highest income possible at a given annuity age. However, it will cease on your death. To get the best income later, it is possible to insure your life for the required inheritable fund value as early as possible. Then on your death, the full value of your fund pays out to your dependants, free of inheritance taxes. It can then be invested tax-efficiently to provide an income.

If this strategy is adopted, it could significantly increase your income in retirement, provide for and protect your beneficiaries and financial dependants and pass capital free of taxes to whomsoever you want. Your pension from your funds will cease on death, but be replaced by more efficient funding – for both income and tax reasons. It is important to have a whole of life policy to do so and companies like Zurich have a guaranteed premium and sum-assured whole-of-life policy on offer. The younger you are when you do this, the cheaper it will be for the rest of your life.

Pension benefits generally

Pension benefits are payable to the member of the pension scheme. The default position for all schemes is that on the death of the member of the pension scheme, pension assets and options pass to a spouse or civil partner, with children as dependant beneficiaries (usually pensions may be paid to a dependant child up to the age of 23, but different funds have different rules). If you are a cohabitee, but not married or in a civil partnership, you will not automatically receive the pension benefits of the member on death. You may have lived with the unmarried partner for 25 years, and even had children by them, but you may still not be entitled to receive their pension benefits. It is therefore important that a letter of wishes be left with the trustees of the pension fund to indicate where the member wishes the benefits to go on their death. Unfortunately this is a discretionary position. What if the member left a former spouse, now divorced, who was financially dependant on him? The trustees may have difficulty with this one, especially where multiple claims may be made by other financially dependant people.

However, there is nothing to state that when you retire you cannot name anyone as your co-annuitant for a joint and survivorship annuity. Note that once this election has been made it is irrevocable, and cannot be changed once you start taking your benefits. This is because the annuity has been calculated on the age of your partner as well as your age. This also causes problems if your spouse or partner has died before you – you cannot add another person later, once the annuity is in payment. Proper planning is essential to maximise annuity and pension options and to avoid paying unnecessary taxes.

Future changes

It may well be that the Government will change the current penal charges and tax penalties applying to pension funds. However, their current thinking is definitely focused on short-term rather than long-term incentives to pension provision. While they concentrate on providing immediate tax incentives to get you funding into pension plans, and equally generous incentives to keep your current pension plan arrangements going, they are nevertheless keen to limit the way in which the benefits of such pensions can be passed to future generations.

In summary, it is evident that the present Government (i) does not want you to pass on pension assets after your death (ii) will apply inheritance taxes and other tax charges to pension funds to ensure that less is passed on death to others (iii) is strictly against the idea of a 'family pension' scenario where the family or third parties can enjoy pension assets from other members in the same pension scheme (iv) is not interested in how the private sector and company funded pension schemes can reduce the burden on State pensions in the future, by using their pension assets for succeeding generations, and (v) has reduced the value of pension scheme protection plans through taking away tax incentives to life cover providing for death benefits where funding has been poor due to not enough time to fund (early death), or reduced lifetime funding.

Many of the flexible benefits introduced through A-Day legislation in 2006 have already, in a short space of time, been overridden. The big opportunity to introduce more flexibility in retirement provision at the retirement and death benefits end of the spectrum have not happened; in fact the reverse is the case.

The Pre-Budget Statement of 9th October 2007 introduced a number of changes affecting pensions and IHT (proposed in the *Finance Bill 2008)*. The statement proposed legislation to ensure that individuals are unable to avoid tax charges by diverting tax relieved pension savings into inheritance using scheme pensions and lifetime annuities; an uplifting of pension credits and measures for employers not to abuse the contribution relief system. The new transferability of NRBs will also assist where a pension scheme would have been subject to IHT, but for the use of the unused portion of a nil rate band of a first dying individual, allowing more taxable assets to be relievable.

In the same statement, the Chancellor closed a loophole for SSAS and SIPP pension schemes where a pension was bequeathed to a family member. A quirk in the rules meant that this was not subject to IHT. From 6th April 2008, if any scheme has less than 20 members, the new rule will apply that any diversion of scheme pensions and lifetime annuities will be subject to unauthorised payment charges and IHT charges. As a SSAS cannot have more than 11 members, SSAS arrangements are brought into line with personal pensions which adopt ASP. The loophole now closed involved surrendering pension rights during their lifetime or reallocating assets after a member's death. This is more fully explained below...

Inheriting tax-relieved pension savings

PBRN 15 states that legislation was introduced in the *Finance Bill 2008* providing that tax-relieved pension savings diverted into inheritance using scheme pensions and lifetime annuities will be subject to unauthorised payment tax charges and possibly inheritance tax. This applies to surrenders made after 10th October 2007 and for increases in pension rights attributable to the death of a member when the member dies after 6th April 2008. Unauthorised payments are subject to income tax charges of up to 70%. Total tax payable could be 82%. The new proposed legislation will

138

not apply where the scheme has 20 or more members and the increases in rights are applied at the same rate for each member. The charge on scheme pensions only applies to 'connected persons', namely family members or business associates. There is no charge if not connected. SSAS schemes can have a maximum of 11 members and could previously pass pension money on to families at death without paying additional tax. The new rules bring SSAS schemes into line with family SIPPs. A SSAS member, on retirement, receives an income direct from the scheme based on actuarial guidelines and is not required to buy an annuity for life using an annuity. On death the remaining assets remain in the pension fund, rather than being lost to an insurance company providing an annuity.

Previously the death of a member did not trigger a tax liability. Now the rules will penalise connected persons (family members or business associates) and schemes of under 20 members passing on pension rights to other scheme members. The tax charge is 70%, in line with tax applied to funds passed on via ASPs. Funds passed on may be liable to inheritance tax, and if the person dies after age 75, could be as high as 82%. There is now a level playing field for ASP and scheme pensions. Planning could involve say an older director without family providing pensions for the rest of the workforce, or the pension funds could go back to the employer after a tax charge of 35%. Note that on death of a member his or her pension fund can still pass to a nominated spouse or civil partner and dependants without penalty where provided for under the rules.

Successive budgets and Finance Acts (2009, 2010) have tightened the noose in respect of pension funding and contributions, but we may see a relaxation of the compulsory ASP age from 75 to 77 in 2012, and possibly a reduction of ASP rules and how income is taken in later retirement.

22

Fee-Based Financial and Retirement Planning

Financial planners charge fees for advice. Brokerage or commission is usually paid as part of the product implementation process. Both advice and implementation functions can be time-costed, and commissions arising could be rebated back into the product purchased, or to the individual or business to whom the product sale is made. From 2012, only fee based options will be available to consumers in respect of pensions and investments – protection products can still be sold on a commission basis.

The two questions probably uppermost in the minds of readers are whether it is worth paying a fee for financial planning advice, and how do you assess the adviser and the quality of the advice to be given? These are difficult questions, especially as many pensions' specialists are good at choosing the right kind of funds for you to invest in, but when it comes to actual retirement and the various options open to them for their clients, they are sadly lacking.

Associations like the Institute of Financial Planning (based in Bristol) have been pushing fee-based financial planning for years, and have a register of certified financial planners. So does the PFS – the Personal Finance Society, incorporating the CII and the LIA, the Life Assurance Association. Those with the CFP, the certified financial planner status, would probably be your best bet, or Chartered Financial Planners from the PFS. Retirement planning, after all, does not only mean dealing with your various pension plans, but encompasses a whole range of investment planning, savings, and ongoing life assurance.

Long-term care possibilities need to be taken into account, and if in business, it may even mean succession planning for the business and other factors. Estate planning and tax planning also form an intrinsic part of the advice process and need to be taken into account.

The move in the financial services industry is that if advice is to be independent, it should be fee based, allowing the client to make his or her own judgment call on what products to select, and whether to use the same advisers or not for later products or services. Others are content to have commission-based advice (as they don't like paying fees), or to have commission offset fee-based advice (which is most common).

However, the preferred route is that fees are for advice, and commissions are payable for the implementation of that advice, if required (or further fees are payable). Both functions require time-costed work to be spent on behalf of the client, and at the end of the day, the process costs must be accounted for.

The average level of fees for a senior financial planner would be in the range of £150 – £200 per hour, and an initial report could cost between £750 and £1,500 depending on the complexity involved. As retirement planning is a process that may take many months or years to complete, some prefer to pay a monthly retainer for ongoing advice.

The typical retirement planning advice process would be as follows:

1. Meeting with client to establish objectives.
2. Client instructions drawn up from the objectives.
3. Terms of Business completed, agreeing to fees or other payment structures. (No advice may be given until Terms of Business are agreed).
4. Data gathering phase, and fact finding, risk profiling.
5. Restatement of objectives and prioritisation in order of importance
6. Research and analysis – existing product details and product provider liaison.
7. Initial report completed.
8. Testing of report suggestions and recommendations.
9. Second report or tiered reporting structure with file notes.
10. Product and service research and analysis, including investments, annuities, further pensions, long term care, estate and inheritance tax planning, wills, life assurance, debt management and personal development.
11. Examination of proposals and key features documentation relating to products and their selection.
12. Implementation of the agreed plan.
13. Monitoring, feedback and follow-up.
14. Restatement of objectives and further report to keep on track.

It is not widely known among prospective clients, exactly what processes are involved in successful financial planning, nor the various compliance features that have to be complied with. The above gives some idea of the processes involved. Without this information, you may think the following merely occurs:

1. Meeting with client.
2. Data gathering.
3. Presentation of report or 'reasons why' letter.
4. You get sold something.

The biggest decisions in your life are made at retirement. A mistake at this stage could spell a financial disaster. You may only have one pension fund, and one tax-free lump sum and if you make the wrong decisions, you have to live with them for the rest of your life.

For example, you may decide at retirement (as you are married or have a partner), that the sensible thing to do is to have a pension or annuity that gives you a pension whilst alive, and then pays a (reduced) pension to your spouse or partner. You want the pension to escalate annually to keep up with the cost of living (at say 3% or the RPI); if both of you die too soon, you want the pension fund to continue for at least a guaranteed period of certainty (payable to dependants or heirs). You feel you could invest a tax-free lump sum better and it also gives you financial control to do so. At retirement, your risk profile changes to more cautious, as you cannot afford to lose your money. You are concerned that you may outlive your money, and may become a 'hoarder' and spendthrift. Typical of most people, isn't it? Sure, because it makes sense to think in this way.

You are also concerned that you may or will lose your entire pension fund value if you die, and it cannot be passed on to your heirs or dependants.

What most people do (well, about 95% of them) is follow the instructions from the product provider on how to purchase their pension or annuity (or if employed, merely accept the pension details from their employer), and certainly for the former, maybe in the wrong type of arrangement, unsuited to their retirement needs. In other words, the advice you get may not be the right advice. What may seem to be perfectly normal to you (to take a pension for yourself and your spouse, with escalating income and guarantees) could also be an inflexible option.

For example, if your partner dies before you, you will be locked into a low-level pension for the rest of your life; whereas what you may want is the ability to increase income in retirement, to have your whole original pension fund pay out on death – instead of losing it – tax-free. Don't merely accept the options given by the product provider. Always ensure that every alternative has been properly thought out before making those all-important decisions.

What if your spouse or partner dies before you? Bad luck, you are still locked in to that annuity rate chosen at the outset to pay for two lifetimes, even though it will now only pay out for one lifetime. Do you have any flexibility or control at all? Not much. You may select a draw-down option, but eventually you must buy an annuity, or have an ASP (alternatively secured pension) at age 75. Have you protected your pension fund value for your heirs? Not likely, as you didn't think it could be done. Have you got the best deal at retirement? Are you a smoker? That last statement could increase your pension annuity payments. Has the whole market place been researched to get you the best open market option, or impaired annuity option? You could significantly increase your income in retirement, and create new lump sums at the same time – if only you knew how.

The pension process described above (two pensions, escalating, paying out for a term certain etc) is the most expensive and inflexible option. The guarantees to be taken out of the pension fund to pay for that 'normal' option can take up to 70% of your fund value, leaving the rest to buy you an income. Modern retirement planning techniques financially engineer you the best deal from your money. You can get a higher income, you can protect your funds for your heirs, you can make the process more flexible, with more options, if correctly advised.

The amount of any fees to be paid, in reality, pales into insignificance, if you are receiving the best retirement and financial planning advice. Everyone, no matter how small they feel their retirement funds are, can improve their positions through proper financial planning.

Our strategies for people entering the actual retirement cycle is to keep them as flexible as possible, as big changes have occurred after A Day on 6th April 2006. You have more flexibility and greater investment options, and above all, more time to consider your options and make your plans.

For example, you do not have to take an annuity from your funds – ever. You can have pension income draw down up to age 75, and beyond – albeit at a reduced level, if you wish. You can pass on pension benefits to your heirs after tax is paid, or divert pension income to family members, or set up pension schemes for them and pay contributions. You can hold qualifying commercial property in your pension scheme, and you can now purchase that commercial property from yourself (as the former connecting provisions have been abolished). You can release capital through your pension fund purchasing your qualifying property (and other assets that are allowable); the result is that when the pension fund sells the asset, there is no capital gains tax to pay and all growth has been tax-free. Contributing your qualifying property to your pension scheme is also tax relievable to you.

Proper planning and advice is therefore essential for most people – if only to consider their options.

23

Death Before Retirement

Should you die 'in service', in other words before retirement, then the pension fund rules will usually stipulate what sort of death benefits are payable and when.

Employers may have death in service benefits, arising from the pension fund itself, or provided by group scheme life assurance. The latter is usually available up to retirement age and then ceases. Group life cover is a multiple of salary, for example two or four times final remuneration, or a fixed amount, and is payable to named beneficiaries or dependants. Payments made by the trustees, for tax reasons, are always discretionary, but a letter of wishes is followed, giving direction for lump sum payments.

If there are no additional group scheme or death in service benefits, then on death before retirement, there would either be a return of current fund value (the better deal), or a return of contributions paid plus say 4% or 5% (worse than a return of current fund value). The differences can be enormous, especially where single premium contributions have been made – as much as 80% less than current fund values. One can approach the pension provider and ask for a change in how and what death benefits are payable – some will charge you to make this change.

Such payments on death before retirement are usually tax-free. Partnership group life schemes provide tax-free benefits on death for all from 9 April 2003 (not just for the first dying).

Dependants' pensions provided on death before retirement will not count towards the standard lifetime allowance. There is technically no limit on benefits which can be provided for dependants on death before retirement. If a pension is paid, there can be no guaranteed periods and no provision for value protection. A spouse and children age under 23 will automatically qualify, as will civil partners. If an unmarried couple – you must provide proof of financial dependency to receive a dependant's pension.

Return of funds and pension contributions and death in service life assurance (including pension term assurance) can be paid tax-free so long as the payments overall are within the standard lifetime allowance, which is £1.8 million in 2010/11, and is frozen at £1.8 million from 2010/2011 to 2015/16.

Lump sum payments in excess of the standard lifetime allowance will be subject to tax at 55% (unless funds were protected under your own PLA, when the higher limits will be paid without penalty).

24

Death After Retirement

Once you have retired from your pension fund, you will be receiving your monthly pension or annuity or drawdown. Your pension funds will have been invested by the pensions' provider to produce an income, and this is generally known as an annuity income. Unless there is a guarantee operating, the main pension itself will come to an end. However, dependants', spouse and civil partner survivors' pensions may be payable until they end on the death of the retiree.

The type of death benefits, if any, will depend on the type of annuity or pensions contract, or other arrangements, such as drawdown, in force at the time.

The most common types are as follows.

Occupational pension schemes

If single, the pension will merely cease. Some schemes have a guaranteed period of payment, and pension payments will continue to the estate of the deceased, or nominated beneficiary or dependant.

If married, usually a reduced pension is payable to the spouse, until his or her death, depending on the scheme rules. 50% widow's or widower's pensions are common, but the range could be from less than that to up to 2/3 of the member's pension.

Personal pension schemes and schemes where annuities are payable

Much depends on the type of the scheme. A scheme with a term certain guarantee will pay out for that term and then cease. For example, if the annuity is payable for two lifetimes, but for a minimum of 10 years, and both annuitants die in, say, year eight, then the annuity continues paying for another two years (to the estate or dependants) before it ceases.

If a single life annuity, then after any guaranteed period, the annuity will cease paying.

If a joint and survivor annuity, then on the first death, the annuity continues paying to the survivor (usually a reduced amount) until the death of the survivor, when it ceases – unless within the term certain guarantee period, if there is one attached. If the spouse dies before the member, then on the death of the member, the annuity will cease unless within a term certain guarantee period.

If a single life nil guarantee annuity is taken, for the highest income option, and the underlying pension fund is insured, then on the death of the annuitant, the annuity itself ceases, but the insurance proceeds pays out in trust outside of the deceased's estate, free of all taxes. This may then be reinvested for income, or for a voluntary purchase annuity which is more tax efficient.

If the situation is a fund in income draw-down, then the following occurs. There are three options for the spouse under draw-down:

1. A return of fund less 35% tax – there is no inheritance tax payable unless it is left to the estate. The option must be taken up within two years of the deceased passing away.
2. The remaining fund buys a single annuity. If the spouse inheriting the pension fund then dies, the fund can be passed on to heirs.
3. To continue with income withdrawal for two years before options (i) or (ii) above. To continue to receive an income until the policyholder would have turned age 75, or the dependant's 75th birthday if sooner. Dependant children under age 18 can also benefit.

If under age 75 and in drawdown, the position is known as an unsecured pension (USP) – as it is unsecured against an annuity. On death before age 75, the remaining funds can be paid as a cash lump sum, subject to a tax charge of 35% or used to provide a pension or withdrawal facility for a dependant. This can be drawn until age 75 in line with the unsecured pension rules. If taking income from a short-term annuity at death, then a full refund is payable less the 35% tax charge. Note that no lump sum is payable from the short-term annuity.

If age 75 and over, draw down will be in an alternatively secured pension (ASP) or an annuity would have been purchased. On death, the value of the plan must be used to provide income for the individual's dependants. The age of the dependants (before or after age 75), will determine whether the pension is secured under the scheme, paid via an annuity, or as unsecured income (USP) if age under 75 – after age 75, the ASP and annuity options are available. If no dependants, the value of the fund can pass to other members of the pension scheme nominated by the member or to a registered charity.

If the funds have been phased (where pension segments have been taken as the individual requires them), then the position is as follows. On death, the full fund can be paid to dependants free of tax. If the transfer was originally from a company scheme, then only 25% may be taken as tax-free cash and the balance as an annuity or an unsecured (drawdown) income. The death benefits are better than draw-down. One can also purchase an impaired life annuity, if required, with higher income.

146

It is unlikely that any death after retirement life cover benefits will be available, unless provided independently by the annuitant.

Payments of lump sum death benefits cease after age 75. However, there are circumstances where they may be paid after age 75. These are payments to a registered charity, transfer lump sum death benefits, on scheme wind up where the dependant's pension entitlement is deemed to be trivial (less than 1% of the SLA); and where a lump sum is paid under a 5-year guarantee right which existed on 5th April 2006.

In most instances, it would be in the interests of all parties to have death benefits paid in trust outside of the estate, to avoid probate before being paid out to beneficiaries.

Transfer lump sum death benefits become unauthorised after 6th April 2007 when the member or dependant dies on or after that date. In addition, the facility to guarantee an ASP for ten years is removed where the member dies on or after 6th April 2007.

25

Long-Term Care

Long-term care will affect 25% of those over age 80, and is an aspect not properly provided for by retirees. As the population ages, demand for long-term care is growing. By 2050 there will be twice as many people aged over 85 and overall costs will increase fourfold. A physical or mental disability could occur at any time, and care may need to be provided in a nursing home or 'in the community' at your own home. A survey commissioned by GE Life in August 2006 found that 80% of retirees have yet to work out how they will meet the costs of care if they become too ill to look after themselves. Around 3 million people currently spend all or some of their last years in care homes, and their families pick up the financial burden. Long term care funding is a growing problem as people live longer with limited state funding and diminishing personal resources. This leads to a financial shortfall in retirement.

The costs of long-term care could financially cripple a retiree, leaving his or her dependants destitute, and using up income and capital to such an extent that nothing is left for one's heirs. The average costs of proper care could run to about £2-3,000 per month, more if acute hospital care is required.

From April 2005, the state will meet the full cost of care where a person's whole assets are less than the lower limit set out below, and proportionate costs where assets are between the lower and upper limits.

	Lower	Upper
England	14,000	23,000
Wales	20,750	22,000
Scotland	13,750	22,500
Northern Ireland	13,500	22,500

Capital and income are means-tested. You first have to use up your own assets and income, before the state, through the local authorities and Department of Work and Pensions, pays for you. You could stay in your house, but when you die, it could be sold to pay for long-term care costs. Over 40,000 homes are dispossessed and sold each year, because of this situation (affecting over 70,000 people).

It is therefore vital that your retirement planning includes planning at all stages of retirement, including the possibility of going into care. The position is worsened if you have to care for an elderly relative. Without adequate lifetime pension and investment funding, savings and long-term care plans become prohibitively more expensive the older you get. As with many people then, you may need more money as you get older, not less.

Long-term care insurance is a fairly recent innovation in the UK market place. It will provide funds to pay for nursing care when you cannot look after yourself, and fail a number of Activities of Daily Living (ADL) tests.

Some policies provide pure insurance, others are investment based, and they are to be found both offshore and in the UK. To claim insurance benefits, the individual must usually be incapable of performing two or three out of five or six ADLs, such as bathing, dressing or feeding oneself. Where the policy proceeds are paid directly to the care provider, then these benefits are tax-free.

Policies can be funded on either a lump sum or a regular premium basis. Some contracts are structured as investments and if no claim is made during the policyholder's lifetime, then the fund is returned. There is no tax relief on the premiums, and the policy may not cover acute conditions (such as major surgery) or some mental illnesses that are difficult to prove.

The Government appointed a Royal Commission that reported in March 1999, and came out strongly in advising people to fund for long-term care. The view appears to be that the Government will fund care but not residential costs in the future, but still has a long way to go.

There is no state assistance where assets exceed the upper limits in the table. These assets do not include the value of your house, but your house can be sold after you die, if no dependant is living in it. Income and capital assessed include everything you have – pensions, most state benefits, savings, investments and possibly your home.

One of your strategies may be to sell the house and to invest the cash to provide for income whilst in care, with a return of the investment to your heirs or dependants on your death. Equity release is proving popular as a means of funding for private care provision. Other planning would involve getting your income and capital into exempt areas. For example, qualifying capital includes property, shares and cash, but not capital held by a discretionary trust. However, one must be careful not to deprive oneself of certain assets, as the authorities could add this back in assessing you.

The main **capital** to be disregarded for the long-term care assessment is as follows:

- the surrender value of a life policy
- the value of one residence under certain circumstances
- proceeds of the sale of any premises formerly occupied
- future interest in property other than in certain land and premises
- gifts in kind from a charity
- personal possessions, including works of art
- certain business assets
- capital not in your name (only your share of a joint bank account can be included)

- certain rights that have not yet crystallised as cash but would have a value to a third party.

The main **income** disregards are as follows:

- income from disregarded capital assets
- income support payments
- income from an annuity
- from personal injury trusts
- from a life interest or life rent
- earnings from outside the UK
- tax payable
- expenses from voluntary or charitable bodies
- up to 50% of your occupational pension if not residing with your spouse or maintaining him or her
- payments by third parties to your living costs
- any income in kind
- certain payments from insurance policies
- council tax benefits
- income support for housing costs
- many other exemptions.

Planning areas would be to invest in qualifying life policies (providing for long-term care if required), planning around the house, equity release, transferring assets to heirs, planning with trusts. However, the wealthy will battle to shelter every conceivable asset, and the better view is to rather utilise all assets to pay for care, thus ensuring private, not state care as being better for you.

Note that different core provisions may apply in Scotland, England, Northern Ireland and Wales.

26

Pensions and Divorce

Divorce happens to a third of the general population at any one time, and pensions have become an important part of the divorce settlement. This is particularly the case where for example, one spouse worked and made 'net relevant earnings' for pension scheme contributions, or enjoyed an occupational pension scheme and its benefits and the other spouse brought up the family, and was unable to be in the workplace.

Not only did that spouse rely on his or her partner for income during their working lifetimes, but also for retirement income. Problems were then bound to arise in the event of divorce or dissolution of a civil partnership as to how the pension fund was to be shared, if at all. The sharing aspect being a difficult proposition may not have been entirely the fault of the member of the pension scheme, though. The rules of the pension fund often meant that pension assets were not divisible for non-contributory, non-pension fund members, and that pension funds before retirement could not be attached for divorce purposes. In addition, HMRC rules were such that membership of a pension fund approved by HMRC, could only be possible under a given set of criteria, and that one who had not satisfied these rules could not own the pension fund. Therefore, the non-income-earning spouse could not share in the fund prior to retirement.

After retirement had taken place, the situation was completely different. It was not a retirement fund in place, but rather a stream of income and that could be attached by the courts. However, the retiree would still have full use of the tax-free lump sum, and also the decision whether to take it or not in the first place. If divorce was being contemplated, the likelihood of a full pension without a tax-free lump sum was a distinct possibly – to deny the other party access to the tax-free lump sum.

The divorcing parties would also still be bound to each other after the divorce had taken place, as the income would be split after the divorce. Divorce reformers favoured a clean break and settlement, and the only way forward was to divide the pension scheme assets before retirement and allow pensions to be taken with each portion, separately.

The other major area of concern had been the fact that a divorced spouse or civil partner was no longer a widow of the deceased pension member and would lose valuable pension benefits if the member died. This was particularly the case when the member remarried or left letters of wishes for the payment of funds to others.

The Welfare Reform and Pensions Act 1999 enabled pensions splitting to occur from 1 December 2000 when divorce settlements are contemplated.

Under a pension splitting or sharing order, there would be a pension debit (a reduction in the value of the pension holder's fund), and a pension credit (the rights allocated to the other spouse or civil partner) in the hands of the former spouse or civil partner. If a money purchase fund, the value of the fund would be reduced by the pension debit. An occupational pension scheme may create a new member's category to cover a former spouse or civil partner, who then becomes a member of the pension scheme in his or her own right. If a final salary scheme, the credit and debit would have to be revalued through to the date of retirement.

Where valuations are concerned, the basis for determining how much the pension credit or debit would be worth is the cash equivalent transfer value, or any other such value as agreed by the Court.

If before retirement, the former spouse or civil partner can transfer the value of the debit to an appropriate pension scheme.

The splitting of pension assets need not be equal, but will in all likelihood tend towards equality. Pension assets may be offset against other assets, depending on the nature of the settlement agreed.

What are the implications for pensions splitting as opposed to income sharing after retirement? The greatest implication would probably be less income for both parties. This is because the husband, usually as the older life annuitant (if all of the fund was available), could receive much higher income to be split with his former spouse. However, if the fund itself was split and then annuities purchased for each party, the lower aged (in this case female) annuitant would receive lower income. However, she would have peace of mind and not be dependant on the former spouse in any way.

The concept of 'earmarking' meant waiting for a share of the ex-spouse's or civil partner's pension on retirement. If he died before retirement, the ex-spouse or civil partner would get nothing. Pensions splitting is certainly better than earmarking, as is sharing the pension fund and becoming an additional member of an occupational scheme fund.

Pre- and post-A Day, the position is as follows

Those with pension credits can apply for an increase in their lifetime allowance to offset the value of the credit (not available if you have applied for Primary Protection). After A Day, there will still be pension debits and credits, but maximum benefits will be based on the lifetime allowance.

Pre-A Day, any pension credit is ignored for the purposes of the donor's lifetime allowance. The value is taken into account to determine the maximum benefits at A Day subject to protection. After A Day, a pension credit will count towards the recipient's lifetime allowance where the rights acquired have not already been tested against the lifetime allowance. Pension debits will not count towards the donor's lifetime allowance.

Bear in mind the state pension for ex-spouses and civil partners. An ex-wife or civil partner can rely on her own contribution record as well as her ex-husband's or civil partner's – but should also look to making Class 3 voluntary contributions, if any shortfall is expected.

27

Pension Mortgages

42% of 61-70 year olds still have a mortgage of some kind to repay and one in eight people of those (12%) have a lifetime mortgage for equity release. The number of people who still have mortgages well into retirement is set to increase.

A pension mortgage is one where the tax-free lump sum arising from the pension plan at retirement is used to repay the mortgage loan outstanding at the date of retirement.

At one time, mortgage providers insisted on a repayment vehicle for interest-only mortgages, no doubt to ensure that they received back their outlay at retirement date. This is no longer as prevalent as in the past, with most mortgage providers leaving their clients to their own repayment devices.

However, using a tax-free pension lump sum as a mortgage repayment investment vehicle can be hugely tax-efficient. This is because the pension contributions made to the pension scheme are tax deductible at your highest rates of tax. The pension scheme then grows tax-free, and depending on the type of scheme, should return on average 25% of the value of the fund as tax-free cash. This in turn means that HMRC has part-funded the purchase of your private home through the tax system.

The danger in the pensions mortgage scheme lay in the fact that the lump sum would not be available to boost retirement income, or reduce debt-traditional methods or usages for the tax-free cash. However, on the other hand, the mortgage would be paid off, thus reducing cash outflows after retirement.

Problems have arisen in the past with HMRC funding limits. Individual's earnings have been unable to sustain the levels of funding required to generate the right amount of tax-free cash required to pay off the entire mortgage, and this may have lead to a shortfall. In addition, the mortgage lender could not enforce the use of the tax-free cash to redeem the mortgage (as it could not take a pension scheme as security), and the use of pension mortgages has largely fallen away.

On the bright side, the pension mortgage did ensure that many people, as homeowners, also had substantial additional pension funds, if they decided not to use their tax-free cash to redeem the mortgage loan, but rather to use it for increased retirement income.

28

Pensions Mis-Selling – What to Do

Pensions mis-selling first came to prominence following Robert Maxwell's misuse of his company pension schemes to fund his business arrangements. Greater scrutiny of all pension funds resulted, and investigations were made into those employees who had transferred out of perfectly good company final salary pension schemes into personal pension plans, mostly to their detriment.

The practice to contract out of SERPS (now S2P) was fuelled by the Government which offered what was essentially a 'bribe' to leave the SERPS (State Earnings Related Pension Scheme) by allowing companies and other employers to pay less in National Insurance to the state by having NI contributions paid into appropriate pension plans for employees contracting out of SERPS. Employees pay 11% of earnings between £110.01 and £844 p.w. plus 1% of all earnings above £844 p.w. The employer contribution is 12.8% of all earnings in excess of the first £110 p.w. If contracted out these rates are reduced by 1.6% for employees and by 3.7% for employees in salary-related schemes (total 5.3%) and 1.4% for employees in money purchase schemes (total 3%). There is also an employee rebate available of 1.6% and employer rebate of 3.7% on earnings between £97.01p.w. to £770 p.w. NI rates increase by 1% from 2012 for both employee and employer.

The bottom line is that it would not normally be beneficial to contract out or leave an occupational pension scheme when both employer and employer contribute, to leave it for one where only the employee is contributing.

At one stage, statistics put forward by life offices favoured better returns through contracting out, but then, after a few years, others brought out statistics stating that those who had contracted out may be better off if they now contracted back into SERPS/S2P. This was particularly the case for older ages.

However, in the interim, life offices were fuelling the contracting out process, and financial advisers were moving employees from final salary and other occupational pensions schemes into personal pension schemes where high commissions were payable, thus further depleting the value of pension funds. During this time, transfer values of pension schemes were also penalised meaning lower values eventuated for the transferee.

A financial services industry outcry followed and the Securities and Investments Board (now the FSA) initiated a lengthy pensions' review process to uncover pension mis-selling. The review process has found that many people were wrongly advised to contract out of their employers' pension schemes and could be re-instated according to the rules that originally applied to them.

If compensation was received for the wrong advice, then the compensation paid was tax-free. Employees could also exceed the 15% limit to make up lost contributions, but the excess over the 15% limit would not receive tax relief. Tax reliefs may be retained by paying back-contributions by instalments.

Pensions' providers and financial adviser firms have been through pension review processes for some years now, and it is unlikely that many of those eligible for compensation or re-instatement have not been contacted to do so.

If any reader has been moved from an employer's pension scheme to a personal pension plan, then contact the product provider of the personal pension scheme to make enquiries as to whether the advice given to do so was correctly given. Failing an adequate response, contact the Financial Services Authority (FSA) on 0845 606 1234, which is their consumer helpline number.

Being wrongly advised to move from an employer's occupational pension scheme into an unsuitable personal pension arrangement is one thing. To properly retire from an occupational pension scheme is another. The two must not be confused. It may be that at retirement, a better income stream can be achieved for you by moving your funds generated by that scheme, to a personal pension scheme to make use of the open market option and other benefits. For example, some occupational pension schemes may not give adequate death benefits, or not allow the class of beneficiary required by the retiree to benefit, after the retiree's death, at the benefit levels that could be obtained elsewhere.

You may have other reasons for leaving an employer's occupational pension scheme, and these may not even be commercial, but important to you. For example, you were made redundant or dismissed from an employer, and do not want to be associated with that former employer under any circumstances – or you have found new employment and joined a new employer's pension scheme, considered better than the one where you were previously. Under those circumstances, it may well be in your personal interests to transfer to the new employer's scheme.

Whatever your personal circumstances, make sure that the numbers are calculated, so that you may be advised properly on your future course of action. Comparisons can then be made and options laid out for you to consider. Hopefully pensions mis-selling is a thing of the past, but one can never be too careful.

29

Building a Suitable Pension Fund

You must decide on your normal retirement date first, then decide what target pension income in retirement is required. Retirement income need not only come from pension funds, it can arise from income from savings and investments as well. If you have a reasonable expectation of an inheritance, or other windfall, then this aspect may also form part of your planning. However, as the latter can never be a certainty, it is wise to treat it as a 'maybe' rather than firm fact, and then to concentrate on building savings and investments.

Also to be taken into account is the following.

1. **Lump sum disbursements at retirement.** For example, paying off debts, or redeeming a mortgage, buying a new car, taking a well-deserved holiday, paying for university fees and other capital expenditures.
2. **Ongoing outflows of income.** Monthly expenditures, regular payments and providing for exceptional out of ordinary small one-off costs.
3. Your **attitude to risk** will determine what sort of funds you will be investing into. A cautious investor will choose low risk investments, a more speculative investor will choose higher-risk investments, but with prospects of capital growth beyond the norm.
4. **Tax efficiency requirements.** Higher rated taxpayers may require investments that reduce or relieve tax (as may those who pay tax at lower levels).
5. **Surplus income and capital available** for investment purposes. It may be that you intend to sell your house at retirement to generate more capital and move to a cheaper house, at home or abroad.
6. **Your investment objectives.** These would include the need for capital growth or income during the initial pre-retirement investment phase, and then possibly a change in investment structure after retirement to provide greater levels of income when you cease work. Also to be taken into account would be the size of target capital required at retirement, its flexibility and accessibility, and whether for retirement only, or perhaps long-term care requirements, provision for dependants and other criteria.
7. **Protection of capital and future retirement funds.** Are the funds required for a single individual, or to pay a pension for a spouse or

partner? Is the avoidance of inheritance tax and general loss of capital at death of retirement funds of great importance?

8. **Your work status.** Whether you are employed, self-employed or unemployed will affect the type of pension funding you may be able to make. Different rules apply to different employment categories when funding for a pension, or making additional pension contributions, and there may be HMRC limits on the level of funding allowed. Whereas previously, if you had no relevant earnings (arising from employment or taxable income from certain categories), you could not make a pension plan contribution. Now, under the stakeholder rules, up to £3,600 p.a. gross (£2,880 net) may be made by anyone, irrespective of how the income arises.

9. The amount of the state **senior citizen's pension** from age 65 for men and 60 for women. (but gradually rising to age 65 and beyond) by 2024).

The above are some of the main factors to be taken into account when deciding on building suitable pension and investment funds. Others may include the fact that some people are distrustful of pensions generally, and do not want to invest in pensions (they fear loss of funds on death, as well as being tied into an annuity purchase at a lower rate for the rest of their lives, and feel they can do better if investing their scarce cash resources elsewhere, with more personal control). Some people may be under the mistaken belief that their employers are taking care of their retirement funding and benefits.

With regard to the two factors mentioned above, there are ways to protect your fund so that you don't lose it on death (which is also inheritance tax effective), and also ways to ensure maximum income from pension funds, even within current strictures. This is the case, even with final salary schemes, that may be poor-performing. Secondly, you must assume responsibility for your own pension funding and do not rely on your employer to ensure your safe and effective retirement. It is up to you, and you alone, to check out your personal situation and to do something about it.

The following table usually excites much interest. You will see what it takes to build a £1 million pension fund, and that the earlier you start, the better. Whilst investment growth is low at present (2010), a good equity or balanced fund could return 10% in the future.

Contributions required at various ages to have £1 million at age 65

Age	Term Years	Contribution p.a. (p.m.)	Interest p.a. (compound)	Value
1	65	£152 (£12.78 pm)	10%	£1m
15	50	£687 (£57.25 pm)	10%	£1m
20	45	£1,265 (£105 pm)	10%	£1m
25	40	£2,055 (£171 pm)	10%	£1m
30	35	£3,355 (£280 pm)	10%	£1m

35	30	£5,530 (£461 pm)	10%	£1m
40	25	£9,250 (£770 pm)	10%	£1m
45	20	£15,900 (£1,325 pm)	10%	£1m
50	15	£28,600 (£2,383 pm)	10%	£1m
55	10	£57,100 (£4,758 pm)	10%	£1m
60	5	£150,000 (£12,500 pm)	10%	£1m

The above assumes no charges, and is shown at one rate of interest (10%) over the term as opposed to the more generally accepted range of 5% or 8%. It also assumes a gross pension contribution at that level, whereas payments are actually made net at 20% tax relief. However, pension tax reliefs may not be around for ever, so the gross return is used. A parent could build a £1million pension fund at age 65 for a child age one now, for less than £13 per month. However, if you are age 40 now then you would need to save £770 per month over the next 25 years for a million pound fund. It will take less time if contributions are tax relievable, or average fund growth exceeds 10% compound per annum.

How much should you be contributing towards retirement income? The minimum is in the region of 10%, but it depends on your age, surplus income, and target fund, and could be as much as 30-40% for much older ages. Almost 1.5 million pensioners live on a retirement income of less than £5,000 p.a. (Prudential Retirement Index) – 42% of pensioners said they needed an increased income to live comfortably. To get an annual income of £23,000 a year, assuming a full basic state pension, you need an annuity that pays £17,000 a year. To reach that level you need a pension pot or savings of £250,000 (£350,000 to inflation-proof it).

Your objective is then to establish exactly what your target funds are going to be. To do this, you must assume a rate of investment growth on your target fund, and also a percentage return of income from the funds, once retirement starts (without eating into capital).

Let us assume you wish to retire at age 65, in 20 years' time, on a target income of £50,000 gross per annum.

Assume also that to earn £50,000 from your fund per year, at say 5% of fund value, then you will need to have a fund worth at least £1 million. [£1 million x 5% = £50,000]

From the table above, you would need to save £1,325 per month to achieve your target income.

The examples that follow will give you an idea of what is involved in building a retirement plan, if employed or self employed.

Example 1

Tom is married and employed by GasElectronics PLC as a middle manager. He is age 45 now. The company operates a final salary scheme. Tom will have 30 years service with the company and can expect a pension based on 30/60ths of his final salary. He will also receive a tax-free lump sum at retirement of 1.5 times his annual pension. Tom is presently earning £28,000 p.a. and his final salary at age 65 is expected to be £50,571(compounded at 3% to age 65). His target income is £50,000 per annum in retirement.

From employer pension:	30/60 (50%) x £50 571 =	£25,286
From tax-free lump sum:	£37,929 x 5% income =	£1,896
From state pension:	£12,359 at age 65 =	£12,977

(£152.30 pw compounded at 2.5% to age 65, using 2009/10 figures)

Total:		£40,159
Shortfall:	(£50,000 – £40,159) =	£9,841
Total:		**£50,000**

Investment lump sum required: £98,410 if invested at 10%; £196,820 at 5% – investment return to give an income of £9,841 at age 65.

Investment solution:
Tom is employed and can also contribute to a personal pension plan or stakeholder personal pension plan alongside his main employer scheme.

Make investments from surplus income.
Taking the worst scenario, Tom would have to plan to fund for a lump sum of £196,820 to be invested at 5% in 20 year's time.

Tom needs to invest gross £388 per month for 20 years at 7% to earn a fund of £196,820. If HMRC was paying 20% of his contribution as Tom pays net into a pension plan, then his net contribution is £310 per month – £3,720 p.a. (HMRC pays £78 per month to equal £388).

Example 2

Lavinia is a married self-employed PR consultant. She is age 45 and wishes to retire at age 65. Lavinia has been contributing to Personal Pension Plans for the last 12 years, although she was previously employed, and has a small employer's pension fund from that previous employment, which was a money purchase fund. The value of her pension plans together is projected at £260,000 at age 60. Her net relevant earnings for the tax year are £48,000 for pension contribution purposes. She expects her earnings to rise with inflation. Lavinia wishes to have a target income of £50,000 at age 65.

Income from pension fund at age 65: (based on 75% of fund at 6% return)	£11,700
Income from 25% tax-free lump sum: (invested at 5% income age 65)	£3,250
State pension at 65: (assume married couple) (£152.30 pw compounded at 2.5% p.a. to age 65, using 2009/10 figures)	£12,977

Total income: (gross)	£27,927
Shortfall:	£22,073
Total:	**£50,000**

Investment solution:

Lavinia has an income shortfall at age 65 of £22,073 p.a. To achieve this income she needs funds of £220,730 invested for income at 10% and £441,460 invested for income at 5% over the period.

1. She can contribute up to 100% of taxable earnings with a minimum of £3,600 into personal pension plan funding. Pension contributions are tax deductible, so the net cost is less 40% tax relief in total.
2. She can make investments from surplus cash. Some of these may be tax relievable, thus reducing her net cost.

Lavinia would need to invest £870 per month gross (£10,440 p.a.) with a growth rate of 7% over 20 years compound to achieve her investment fund target of some £441,460. This would be a net contribution of £696 per month assuming a pension fund contribution with HMRC contributing £174 (20% of £870).

The cost is further reduced as a higher rate taxpayer by another 20% of the gross amount (20% x £870 = £174), so the cost to her is £522 per month (£6,264 per annum).

Note that 25% of her pension fund would give tax-free cash, so if Lavinia wanted to use part of her funds for tax-free cash investments, she may do so. It has been assumed that the return from the pension fund and returns from tax-free cash are not the same. Note that investment returns should be monitored and if long-term averages are below those expected, then greater funding levels are required.

Building a suitable pension fund therefore requires a calculation taking into account your *target income at retirement age*. One has to work backwards from this position, taking into account existing funds and their projected returns, from all sources. Do not make the fatal mistake of believing your pension fund will get you to your target income alone. If on a '60ths' occupational pension scheme, for example, you will need 30 years of unbroken service with the same employer to achieve 50% of your salary at retirement. In Tom's case, he needed to invest 3,936/28,000 or 14.06% net of his annual income to achieve his target. In Lavinia's case, she needed to invest 6,264/48,000 or 13.05% net of her income currently to achieve her target.

The message is clear – the younger you start, the less there is to make up at the end of the process. It is possible to build significant retirement funds if committed and dedicated to the process. Not all of these need to be in pension funding; savings and investments from all sources will be useful adjuncts.

30

Retiring Abroad

Many retirees, sick of British winters, seek warmer climes for their retirement years, or to be near family, or for many other reasons. Currently, the older you get, the greater the chance of something medically going wrong with you, and the need for quick and speedy medical attention. France, Germany and Belgium have been popular destinations for those wanting rapid medical treatment and higher standards of care, and no doubt these considerations feature in the retirement plans of many.

Wherever your retirement destination, how you manage your financial affairs and money is going to be an important consideration. For example, should you purchase that flat in Spain, owning it directly, or through an offshore company? Passing shares in the company to heirs and dependants could be more tax efficient than passing property in other countries.

Whether you should take your investments with you, and invest them in the new country of residence, or leave them in the UK, or maybe transfer them to an offshore tax haven, make use of trusts to stream income and protect capital, and a host of other considerations need to be taken into account.

Then there are the personal considerations. Will you meet new friends? Should you take a car with you, or buy one there? What if you don't like where you are going and want to come back? Do you keep your investment and tax shelter positions, or do you change them?

The only certainty about life is that it will be subject to change, and one must be prepared to make the necessary adjustments accordingly.

Depending on where you retire to, will determine how your money should be invested, and on what basis. For example, if you lived in the UK all your life and then retired abroad, then ordinarily your residency status and possibly your domicile will change. Residency and domicile are important concepts for tax and inheritance tax reasons. You may have decided to live in Spain (so you are now ordinarily resident in Spain), but decide to be buried in the UK if you die, making your domicile still the UK. That means wherever your assets are in the world, they will be subject to UK inheritance tax. So residency and domicile planning will be important to you.

If you are resident, ordinarily resident and domiciled in the UK, then all of your investment income is taxable in the UK. If you are resident and ordinarily resident, but not UK domiciled, then offshore income arising will only be taxed in the UK if you bring it in to the UK. If you are not resident or ordinarily resident, and no matter what your domicile is, then investment income is not taxed in the UK.

A new tax regime from 6th April 2008 applies to non domiciliaries who are adult and UK resident in the current tax year, and have been UK resident in seven out of ten tax years and will be taxed on the arising basis (not remittance basis as previously) and pay a £30,000 remittance basis charge per annum. There is a *de minimis* level of £2,000 of unremitted foreign income or gains, when the remittance basis will apply automatically without the tax charge.

Planning requires great care so as not to be subject to anti-avoidance tax legislation. The best solution would be to have income producing assets in a low-tax country (or offshore tax haven), received by you in such a way as to pay as little tax as possible. In addition, for capital growth to accrue tax-free and not be subject to estate or inheritance taxes.

You may require new wills for your assets. Some people have a will for the new country of residence/domicile and assets situated there, and another will for UK assets, for example.

Retiring abroad may be a new adventure, but proper planning is most important to avoid elephant traps which may be waiting for you. The general trend of becoming non-resident and non-domiciled, is to invest offshore and to take income from that source as required. If you can capitalise your income and take irregular capital payments, then so much the better as capital is usually not taxable. People also forget that the UK itself can be a tax haven, and many people invest in the UK's investment structures and portfolios.

Realising assets in the UK may give rise to capital gains tax. If you intend to live abroad for at least 5 years, and sell the assets giving rise to the gains once you have moved, then no capital gains tax should be payable. If it is payable, capital gains tax is an optional tax and may be deferred under certain circumstances, forever. In other words, it can die with you if properly planned for.

If considering retiring abroad then, undertake a retirement audit with a certified planner specialising in those types of clients. Best advice early on can save much money later, let alone time spent in trying to rectify things.

Transferring pensions overseas

The transfer by people emigrating or intending to emigrate of their pension schemes to Qualifying Recognised Overseas Pension Schemes (QROPS) is a legitimate transfer allowed by HMRC. For UK residents transferring pensions using QROPS it can be done, but the rules are very complex and advice is required as UK legislation and rules will still apply in most instances, contrary to what is advised by some transfer specialists.

31

Steps in the Pensions/Retirement Process

With the advent of stakeholder pensions, the first step in the retirement planning process could be when you are born. Children now qualify for a pension scheme, even if they have no earnings. Contributions made also qualify for tax reliefs, even though the individual may not be a taxpayer, as contributions are made 'net'. This means HMRC pays the basic tax of 20% (2010/11) directly into your plan. Higher rate taxpayers claim an additional 20% of their net contribution through their tax returns or changes to their tax coding.

The totality of what you decide to do will always come down to how much you can afford to contribute to retirement planning to ensure a financially successful retirement. If you start early enough, it may be as little at 10% per annum – if you leave it too late, it could eat up the whole of your pay package. Between these two extremes would be a reasonable funding well within your financial affordability.

The problem is that early working years are where you earn much less than later in life, and have higher costs, especially with mortgages, school fees and other costs that you may not have in later life, when you would be earning at higher levels. The result is that the magic effect of compound interest has a shorter period to run to help build up your funds. It is therefore important to have a simple strategy and to begin planning immediately – no matter at what stage in the retirement planning cycle you happen to be in right now.

The simplest approach is to set a retirement date for normal retirement, for example, if you wish to cease working at age 60 or 65, or at least slow down and smell the roses.

Then, you will need to set a target income in retirement. If you believe that all debts (like mortgage, car HP, etc) will be paid off at that date, and that you can manage on a set percentage of your final salary, then that is a starting point. Bear in mind that to set a target income based purely on the maximum pension you may receive, could well leave you short of cash at retirement.

For example, if you worked for the same employer for a maximum of 40 years, the maximum pension to be expected would be 2/3 of your final salary, and if you joined a scheme after 1987 then that could be capped at the pensions cap, which was £105,600 in 2005/06. That means you cannot have a pension from HMRC approved funds of more than 2/3 of £105,600 i.e. £70,400. The pensions cap no longer applies after A Day, the 6th April 2006. Schemes prior to 1987 are not subject to the pensions cap. The pensions cap also applied to personal pension plans and money purchase schemes (or defined contribution schemes) prior to A Day.

There is a danger of merely taking HMRC limits as being your maximum levels of retirement income, rather than planning for a true end benefit approach. In other words, how much do I need in retirement, and how am I going to get there?

Retirement planning is not only about pensions. It is also about savings and investments, mitigating taxes, planning for long term care (during retirement) as a possibility, estate planning – making sure there is enough capital in your estate and that your wills are in order, and other areas. It may well include selling the business as a business owner and investing the proceeds, and providing for dependants or a divorced former partner.

Planning also includes making sure that you receive the maximum state pension at age 60 for women and 65 for men (but changing in the future to equalise at age 68), and if you have lived abroad and are presently only entitled to a reduced pension, that you consider paying additionally into the state system to increase or maximise your state pension.

The retirement process

1. Pre-earnings phase – usually age 0-18
2. Earnings Phase – usually age 18 to 65. Investment process begins.
3. Retiring phase – can be from age 50 to age 75 (also the annuity and draw-down option phase)
4. Retirement phase – time spent in retirement
5. Long term care – optional phase for 25% of those over age 80
6. Death benefits phase
7. Re-investment for dependants phase

The retirement funding and financial process

Financing phases in sequence	Period
1. Retirement fund and investment accumulation	Working Life
2. Retirement countdown with accelerated accumulation of funds	10 yrs before retirement
3. Decisions at retirement date for best preservation options	At retirement date

4. Retirement income and investment management   In retirement

5. Providing for long term care from retirement funds if health deteriorates   During retirement

6. Asset and income re-distribution providing for dependants and heirs   On death

7. Reinvestment for income and capital growth   After death

More and more people are thinking of retiring early, and with people living longer, you could spend as much time in your retirement, as you did working. At the turn of the 19th century, the average life expectancy of a male was only 49 years, and for a female, 52 years. By the turn of the last century (2000), the average ages had increased to 75 for males and 79 for females. In a hundred years, the life expectancy has nearly doubled. The question is not that we will live forever, but that we will be retired for much longer than ever before. Our own surveys amongst those who have retired indicate that the biggest fear is not so much the fear of a poor investment risk anymore, but more a fear of outliving your capital and therefore your income.

Retirement is a negative perception. We all know it will happen, and some of us even know when, but we still fail to provide for it adequately, because when we were younger, there were always more important purchases to make and money commitments to be borne than to think about retirement planning. As we get older, perhaps we now feel unable to do anything about it, so let life take its course and hope for the best. Sadly, the state will only provide the bare bones of retirement income – for the rest 'if it's to be, it's up to me'.

The bottom line is that each individual must take responsibility for his or her own retirement planning. Don't rely on your employer, or the Government, they are programmed to provide the absolute minimum.

The steps in the retirement process

Step 1
Set a retirement date (you don't have to keep to it, or even leave employment at that date, even if you mature your pension schemes).

Retirement date: £ _____

Step 2
Set a target income for retirement.

Target annual income: £ _____

Step 3

Decide if that income will escalate or not. Whilst inflation in the UK is around 0-2% in June 2009, it has been in double figures in the past.

Escalation: _____%

Step 4

Work out what average investment growth can be expected (be conservative, possibly at, say, 5% over the next 10-20 years):

Investment growth @: _____%

Step 5

Establish what funds will be available at retirement date: £ _____

Step 6

Establish what income will be available from pensions: £ _____

Step 7

Establish what income will be available from savings and investments (from the funds in step 5):   £ _____

Step 8

Establish what the state pension income will be at retirement: £ _____

(In 2010/11 it is £97.65 p.w. for a single person; £156.15 p.w. for a married couple/civil partnership. Increases each September with inflation figure as at April of that year. From 2011 to increase with earnings, prices or 2.5% if higher).

Step 9

Work out any shortfall between what is expected as target income and actual income [Step 2 minus (Step 6 + Step 7 + Step 8)].

Shortfall in income: £ _____

Step 10

Calculate the size of fund required to produce the extra income. Assume income is, say, 5% of that fund value per annum.

Size of fund: £ _____

Example

1. Age 65, in 20 years time
2. £50,000 p.a.
3. 3% escalation
4. 5% p.a.

5. £300,000 from tax-free lump sums and sale of house
6. £16,000 p.a. at age 65
7. £15,000 p.a. at 5%
8. £13,305 (current married state pension escalated at 2.5% over 20 years)
9. £50,000 – (£16,000 + £15,000 + £13,305) = £5,695 p.a.
10. £113,900 x 5% = £5,695
   (Take £5,695 x 10 = £56,950. Then multiply by 2 = £113,900)

The value of the fund will have to be higher to provide for any escalating income required, or the fund investments will have to provide this additional annual income.

In this case, a fund is required of £113,900 to provide for the shortfall in income of £5,695 p.a. in 20 years time. Adjustments should also be made for inflation, which reduces the value of money in real terms. Add inflation figure to step 10.

Step 11

Decide on how the extra funding will occur. This could be from making additional pension fund contributions, or savings and investments from surplus income, the sale of shares or sale of a property, or maturing endowment policy.

Step 12

Break this down to 'bite-size chunks'. The following table will assist you to find the amount that you need to save each month to the target retirement date on a compound interest basis. The assumption is 10% growth net of all charges and taxes. On the table, find the number of years to your retirement and read off the monthly contribution that will yield £10,000 on retirement. All you have to do then is divide the fund by £10,000 and multiply it by the contribution rate.

Amount required to produce £10,000 worth of funds at any given period to retirement date

Years to retirement	Monthly contribution (£)
1	798.00
2	380.00
3	241.00
4	172.00
5	130.00
6	103.00
7	84.00
8	69.50
9	58.50
10	50.00

11	43.00
12	37.00
13	32.50
14	28.50
15	25.00
16	22.00
17	19.50
18	17.50
19	15.50
20	14.00
21	12.50
22	11.00
23	10.00
24	9.00
25	8.00
26	7.50
27	6.50
28	6.00
29	5.50
30	5.00
31	4.50
32	4.00
33	3.70
34	3.30

Example

The fund required was £113,900
Divide by £10,000 = £11.39
Multiply by the factor for 20 years (in this case), which is £14
£11.39 x £14 = £159.46 needs to be saved each month to reach the fund target of £113,900 in 20 years time.

At retirement

At retirement, there are again a number of steps in the process. In fact, many of these steps should be taken in the 6-12 months at least before retirement, so that you have taken the necessary actions prior to the actual retirement date.

Step 1

Analyse pension funds. Decide on best retirement route. The choice would be from:

- If employed – obtain pension fund details for annual pension, tax-free lump sum, annual pension escalation, death in service benefits, fund transfer value.

- If self-employed, or with personal pension plans, money purchase defined contribution type schemes, then you have a number of options, such as:
  i) conventional retirement, using annuities or
  ii) phased retirement, using a mixtures of annuities and income draw-down, or
  iii) income draw-down from existing pension funds to age 75, then to take an annuity or alternatively secured pension (ASP).

Decide what sort of pension or annuity or income scheme to have. Is it a single pension, or must it pay out for two lifetimes (you and your spouse or partner)? Do you want guarantees? Must it pay out a pension or annuity monthly in arrear or advance, or quarterly, six-monthly or annually? Do you wish for your funds to be capital protected? This means that the balance of your funds (or more) is returned to your estate on death, or in trust for your heirs and dependants, free of all taxes. On your death, do you want a 50% pension for the survivor, or a 2/3 pension?

Step 2

Consolidate pension funds, and check transfer values against the best available open market option (best rate from best annuity provider).

If in an occupational pension scheme, it may also pay you to shop around. Obtain a transfer value from your pension scheme. You could do better than what is being offered from the occupational pension scheme. However, if you do decide to transfer for a better deal, make sure death benefits, pension escalations and other benefits are comparable. Some people transfer from occupational pension schemes to obtain better dependants' benefits for example.

Step 3

Check the basis of death benefits payable by pension funds. The worst type could be 'return of premiums plus, say, 4% or 5%', whereas a return of fund value is better. You can get the product provider to change the basis of death benefits on application, but there may be a fee charged for doing so.

Step 4

Check for annuity guarantees written into the policy documentation. Some product providers could guarantee to pay at a rate of 10-14% or more, and you may lose out by transferring the fund, even under the open market option.

Step 5

If a smoker or medically challenged, get yourself underwritten for an 'impaired life' annuity rate. You could significantly increase your income in this way. If in an occupational pension scheme, the reverse could happen. Because of your medical condition, you may have to take early retirement, and would be penalised, receiving looo pension. If the fund was transferred to an impaired life underwriter, you could significantly increase your pension income, depending on your condition, although other factors, such as the pensions cap, could be a limiting factor.

Step 6

Determine your investment risk and strategy at retirement. Is it the same as before retirement date? Are you now more cautious with your money, because you have stopped work, with less income or none coming in from other sources? Should you adopt a higher risk profile on some of your capital for prospective increased returns?

Step 7

Examine your existing investment portfolio closely to see that it meets with your objectives. Also determine how your tax-free cash lump sums will be invested. Are the investments required as part of your income objectives, or merely for additional capital growth?

Step 8

Reduce or eliminate as much debt at retirement as is possible.

Step 9

You may need to replace lost life cover, particularly if death in service benefits ended at retirement. This should be done in expectation of retirement, and as early as possible. The younger you are, the cheaper it is. Some retirement schemes protect retirement pension capital with life policy guarantees, and this may be an opportunity to increase life cover if required. If adequately funded and with no liabilities or inheritance taxes, you would need less life cover.

Step 10

Once your objectives have been established, and you have consolidated your retirement position, you can take various actions to physically retire. You will have made your choices and taken your options, some of them irrevocable. It is now time to 'smell the roses' and to enjoy your retirement years.

How to get help

There is a lot to do prior to retirement, and you must be certain that you are on the right track. Mistakes could be costly. You may need someone to give your retirement plan the 'once over', or have a financial planner give you guidance. Be prepared to pay a fee for this.

During retirement

The main steps to be taken during retirement will be to monitor your investment portfolios, and to make changes where necessary. There will also be decisions to be made regarding pension policies maturing at different dates, further investment of tax-free lump sums, as well as annuity purchases from time to time.

You may also have to provide for long term care, sometimes residential, at other times incorporating frail care with medical facilities, as part of your later retirement strategy. This may require you to have specific types of investments that protect your assets should you have to go into care. For example, if the state pays for care costs, it could dispossess your house at a later date. You can protect against this, if it arises, but planning is required.

Retirement is not only about the money. You may have personal development plans to keep yourself active, and developing other interests may be important to your well-being.

If a spouse or partner dies

If death occurs during retirement, then this is traumatic enough, without having to worry about sufficient income and capital for those left behind. Ensure that your wills are up to date and that your personal financial affairs are in order at all times. Life policies underwritten in trust are useful because the proceeds are payable directly to beneficiaries through the trust, without having to wait for probate, which could be a blocker on funds required from the estate. Check also your existing policies to see if they are underwritten in trust or not, so that the appropriate steps may be taken before the event occurs to ensure the proceeds are directed to where you want them to go.

Develop an action plan

Planning for retirement and the steps in the process given above are not conclusive. What has been given is a broad- brush approach to get you on a track towards successful retirement. Everyone's circumstances are different and the steps in their individual processes will differ accordingly. If you have an action plan and a strategy with a check- list, then you can keep yourself on track.

32

Who Can Help You with Pensions Questions?

You may have technical queries requiring answers, or retirement planning questions that need answering. Obviously your first port of call will be your pensions advisers and financial planners, and if you do not have one, then call the author's advice line on either 01743 360827, or email tony@tonygranger.com where your queries will be answered.

Retirement planning countdown seminars are held regularly and there is literature on many topics provided by product providers as well as from one of the many annuity services available to assist you with your retirement and pensions planning.

Epilogue

Pensions Simplified as a book was written to satisfy the needs of ordinary people looking for simple answers to the myriad pensions and retirement planning questions and strategies that need to be taken into account to ensure a successful and financially independent retirement. Generally speaking, books on the subject tend to be either highly technical with few practical answers, or too general in nature. For example, you may be advised that if you haven't prepared well enough for sufficient income in retirement, the solution is to only eat two meals a day and move to a smaller house as being the answer to not having enough pension funding in place!

Investments should be safe, meaning in the building society or bank, and be prepared to lose your retirement capital from pension funds to the product providers when you die.

In reality, this type of solution benefits no one. There has been no planning to speak of, and the result is seen as fatalistic. The alternative would be set objectives for retirement, to plan the result of your endeavours, to get the best income possible, to ensure that you have capital growth for the longer term, and to protect your fund capital, as well as your heirs and dependants.

You no longer have to purchase an annuity from age 75 (age 77 from 2012) and can continue receiving pension income in a reduced form of drawdown for those with money purchase schemes. Taking an annuity at retirement still remains an option though, and much progress has occurred in respect of returning annuity surpluses and achieving investment growth through an annuity.

However, this may be adding additional risk to your income streams (if a unit linked or with profits annuity, or whatever). In fact the annuity problem can be largely overcome, even where there are declining interest rates, through other means, such as medically underwriting annuitants for higher annuities, taking guarantees away from the annuity itself (guarantees could cost up to 70% of the value of your funds), and instead insuring the fund, and other mechanisms.

Many people are worried that their pension funds are not protected in retirement from dying too soon. They have cause to be worried. Traditionally annuity providers take the surplus funds on death of the annuitant. However, in some countries, annuity surpluses are paid to the estate of the deceased annuitant, and the UK is seeing the first annuity products promising to do just that. However, there has been no general statement from the pensions' product providers on this iniquitous issue to date, and rather than have the cost of insuring your fund to return capital, there should be a mechanism whereby the product provider does so. This should also apply to final salary schemes and similar funds.

Pensions Simplified has focused on the different types of pension plans available, their structure and uses. Much has been said about the new contribution funding limits and other changes. A core development in the pensions industry, following the regulator's and journalists' endeavours in this area has been the simplification of pension funds and their investment components and charging structures. This has lead to a decrease in new pension funds' cost structures, and greater value for money when taking out new pension funds. Many product providers are working within the 1% cost structure prescribed for stakeholder pensions, for all their funds, and the consumer pensions' purchaser is the winner.

Whilst the pensions' legislation remains complicated, pensions products are becoming easier to understand and simple in their construction. They are also becoming cheaper, with a shift from commission-based advice towards fee-based retirement planning in general.

Financial planners have a great responsibility to ensure that their clients not only get the best deal for retirement, but are adequately prepared for their retirement journeys and for what lies beyond. However, the challenge is equally that of the reader, to ensure that the advice he or she receives is adequate, and that mistakes are not made in the preparation process.

Pensions Simplified should go a long way to assist those planning for retirement by explaining in easy to understand terms, the various processes involved.

Tony Granger
Shrewsbury

Abbreviations

A Day	Pensions reform starts from 6th April 2006
ADLs	Activities of Daily Living
AEI	Average Earnings Index
AA	Annual Allowance
AVC	Additional Voluntary Contributions scheme
ASP	Alternatively secured pension, after age 75
CAT	Charges, Access, Terms
CFP	Certified Financial Planner
CII	Chartered Insurance Institute
COMPS	Contracted Out Money Purchase Scheme
COSR	Contracted Out Salary Related Scheme
DB	Defined Benefits – occupational pension scheme
DC	Defined Contribution – occupational and other pension scheme
EBT	Employee Benefit Trust
EFRBS	Employer Funded Retirement Benefit Scheme
EPP	Executive Pension Plan
FA	Finance Act
FSA	Financial Services Authority
FSAVC	Free Standing Additional Voluntary Contribution scheme
FURBS	Funded Unapproved Retirement Benefit Scheme
GAD	Government Actuary's Department
GMP	Guaranteed Minimum Pension
GPPP	Group Personal Pensions Plan
HMRC	Her Majesty's Revenue and Customs
HP	Hire Purchase
HRP	Home Responsibilities Protection
IPA	Individual Pension Account
ISA	Individual Savings Account
LEL	Lower Earnings Limit
LIA	Life Insurance Association
MFR	Minimum Funding Requirement
MP	Money Purchase
NEST	National Employment Savings Trust
NI	National Insurance
NPSS	National Pension Saving Scheme
NRE	Net Relevant Earnings
OEIC	Open Ended Investment Plan
OMO	Open Market Option
PA	Per Annum
PCLS	Pension commencement lump sum – tax-free cash
PFS	Personal Finance Society
PIPPA	Plan where pension fund is insured

Abbreviations

PPP	Personal Pension Plan
PW	Per Week
RA	Retirement Annuity
RPI	Retail Prices Index
SAA	Special Annual Allowance
Sec 32	Pension policy to accept occupational funds on transfer
SERPS	State Earnings Related Pension Scheme
S2P	State Second Pension
SIPP	Self-Invested Personal Pension Plan
SPP	Stakeholder Pension Plan
SSAS	Small Self- Administered Scheme
SLA	Standard Lifetime Allowance
TA	Taxes Act 1988
TFC	Tax-free Cash
UAP	Upper Accrual Point
USP	Unsecured Pension – drawdown funds before age 75
UURBS	Unfunded Unapproved Retirement Benefit Scheme
VCT	Venture Capital Trust

Index

For further confidential information on pensions options, send this page to:

Retirement Strategies
11 Melbourne Rise
Bicton Heath
Shrewsbury
SY3 5DA

Name _____

Address

_____

_____

_____

_____

Postcode _____

Telephone: _____

Fax: _____

Email: _____

Post to the address above, fax to 01743 240381, or email to
tony@tonygranger.com

Please photocopy this page to avoid spoiling your book